# Better Homes and Gardens®

**Bathroom PLANNER**

Better Homes and Gardens® Books
Des Moines, Iowa

Better Homes and Gardens® Books
An imprint of Meredith® Books

*Bathroom Planner*
Editor: Paula Marshall
Writer: Amber Barz
Contributing Editor: Diane A. Witosky
Designer: David Jordan
Copy Chief: Terri Fredrickson
Managers, Book Production: Pam Kvitne, Marjorie J. Schenkelberg
Contributing Copy Editor: Carol Boker
Contributing Proofreaders: Nancy Dietz, Sue Fetters, Susan Sanfrey
Contributing Technical Reader: Ray Kast
Contributing Illustrator: The Art Factory
Indexer: Kathleen Poole
Electronic Production Coordinator: Paula Forest
Editorial and Design Assistants: Kaye Chabot, Mary Lee Gavin, Karen Schirm

Meredith® Books
Editor in Chief: James D. Blume
Design Director: Matt Strelecki
Managing Editor: Gregory H. Kayko
Executive Editor, Home Decorating and Design: Denise L. Caringer

Director, Sales, Special Markets: Rita McMullen
Director, Sales, Premiums: Michael A. Peterson
Director, Sales, Retail: Tom Wierzbicki
Director, Book Marketing: Brad Elmitt
Director, Operations: George A. Susral
Director, Production: Douglas M. Johnston

*Better Homes and Gardens® Magazine*
Editor in Chief: Karol DeWulf Nickell
Executive Building Editor: Joan McCloskey

Meredith Publishing Group
President, Publishing Group: Stephen M. Lacy

Meredith Corporation
Chairman and Chief Executive Officer: William T. Kerr

Chairman of the Executive Committee: E. T. Meredith III

# Contents

# Capture Your Dreams

## Planning the perfect bath begins with creating a wish list.

Everyone starts and ends their day with a trip to the bath. This room, however, is often stylistically and spatially neglected: It's often a few functional plumbing fixtures tucked into an exceptionally small room—not exactly a mood brightener!

For your bathroom building project, think beyond the basic box. Bathrooms can be open to the sun and the sky, a favorite garden, or a morning coffee bar. Match the style of your new bath to the personalities of its daily users, not to what you think a few visitors might expect to see. Keep track of even the most far-fetched ideas. Clever thinking might provide you with the perfect solution.

This book is designed to guide your dreams toward creating a workable plan, whether that involves incorporating a dreamy whirlpool tub or adding a powder room for convenience.

Inspiration is in every photograph, practical advice to move you through the planning process on every page. So draw a hot bath, toss in a rubber duck for company, and flip through these pages to begin your project.

**Right:** The bathroom is the most personal room in the house, so make it a place you like to be. Add special accessories such as candles and good towels to create a feeling of comfort. Include a few things to personalize the space: artwork, flowers, or a favorite scent. Of course, include fixtures and features that suit your bathing needs and preferences. Whirlpool baths such as this one make lingering in the tub a delight, and a bather can take in the view or enjoy a fire.

A master bath can be small and still feel luxurious. White fixtures, generous-size windows, and a neutral palette combine with gold-color accents to offer this 9x13-foot master bath an air of elegance. The bath features raised vanities, an oversize tub, and a separate glass-enclosed shower. Thinking first of the desired luxury allowed this homeowner to find creative solutions to fit it all in a relatively small space.

# What's Your Style?

Before choosing the plumbing fixtures, even before setting the budget, think about style. After all, once all those practicalities enter the picture, truly indulgent thoughts are overshadowed by facts and figures . You needn't be overly specific, just think of the images and words that convey the abiding intent of your bathroom project: a spot of luxury, joyful colors, quiet repose, traditional elegance—whatever suits you. Use your style to guide all the choices you'll make in creating a plan.

**Above: Trust your instincts.** Here, apricot-glazed walls soften the crisp, colorful zig-zag chair rail tiles that surround the fluted corner sink. The homeowner designed the lighthearted, colorful bath herself.

**Left: Think of your favorite things for inspiration.** Soft greens combined with buff-color limestone set a tranquil tone for this bath. The inspiration for this bath comes from a favorite piece of artwork. For this complicated remodeling project, the homeowners used an interior designer and architect to transform art to artful reality.

# Match Form to Function

**Below: Think light thoughts.** Interior light in this bath is maximized by replacing solid interior walls with spans of glass. Light flows between the exterior bedroom and the interior bath via clerestory windows. Sinks are topped with separate mirrors to keep the rectilinear design going.

Often a bathroom project starts because the space is dysfunctional: Even two people can create a crush trying to share a tiny mirror and sink to simultaneously prepare themselves to meet the day. Or an awkwardly placed tub allows no room to turn around and towel off after bathing. Consider all the functions required of a space. Then tackle the puzzle of trying to fit all the elements into the existing space. If, after all the math is done, there simply isn't enough room, look at the adjacent spaces. You may be able to "steal" a few precious square feet from a hallway or closet.

A clever architectural solution, this spacious master bath is enclosed in a bump-out on the home's second floor. The bump-out functions on two levels, holding the tub and shower and also serving as a covered entry on the main level.
Below: Borrowing space from the master closet provided room for this gracious granite-top double vanity.

Combining a sewing room with the former master bath created this luxurious space at little additional cost. Diamond-shape insets create a "rug" on the cool, white tile floor. The nostalgic light fixture draws attention to the new vaulted ceiling and lights the room's focal point, a reproduction claw-foot tub.

# Be Selective

Not only does every square inch of a bathroom work hard, the overwhelming number of choices in adding or revamping a bath can make it seem like every square inch requires a different choice. Approach the task by category: surfaces, cabinetry, and fixtures. To balance the budget you may have to cut costs in Column B to get what you want in Column A, but this approach helps keep the task manageable. Some basic construction costs may be less flexible. Items such as running new plumbing lines, replacing windows, and building walls will lead the budget. Determine the must-have items at the start.

**Above: A skylight in the shower replaces the natural light lost from an attic window that was covered to make room for the shower. Green ceramic tile shower walls blend nicely with the green marble and cream French limestone floor. A marble-topped cherry vanity is appointed like fine furniture with hinged brass handles and paneled doors.**

Left: **Think of comfortable rooms as you dream. Widely spaced fixtures, wicker chairs, and an armoire create a furnished look reminiscent of a living room in this bath. The huge freestanding tub is positioned as a sofa might be, basking in the light and views of a bay window dressed with draperies and valances.**

Antique furnishings mix with reproduction fixtures to create a charming vintage bath. The custom-made marble vanity top, porcelain sink, and brass vanity stand fit the space.

# Play the Numbers

Whether creating an entirely new space or revamping an old one, consider the bathroom's layout from the floor up. Minimum clearances ensure less banging of elbows and doors; well-placed natural and artificial lighting helps family members put their best face forward; and safety is always a top concern. Storage? Since there never seems to be enough, figure out what you need—and then add plenty more wherever space allows.

**Right:** Universal design is a philosophy, not a style. A working stoplight adds lively color to this accessible bath. The tile floors have the right amount of grip for wheelchair maneuvering. All the plumbing fixtures are equally accommodating. The sink provides plenty of leg room and is fitted with easy-to-operate anti-scald faucets.

The ultimate design compromise, a half-wall offers modest separation between the vanity and tub. A shelved niche doubles the function, providing storage for towels, toiletries, and other items. The ledge on top is ideal for display.

## WILL A HALF-WALL WORK IN YOUR BATH?

The National Kitchen and Bath Association recommends that you allow a minimum clearance of 16 inches from the centerline of the toilet to a wall (or any other obstruction) on both sides. Walls adjacent to the toilet also should be reinforced to receive grab bars. For a listing of the current NKBA guidelines, see Chapter 6, "Elements of Good Design," beginning on page 110.

# Gallery of Style

More than a place to brush your teeth and comb your hair, a new bath can express personal style and pamper every need.

**Right: Sandstone countertops, pine trim, and wide-plank pine floors give this bath an old-fashion flavor. A pleasing peeling-paint finish on the louvered vanity cabinet doors contributes to the aged look. Positioned between the two sinks, a double-side, metal-frame, swivel mirror offers a touch of privacy without blocking communication.**

Just like a long soak in a luxurious whirlpool tub, your bathroom should offer a look that relaxes and renews—whether you're waking up to start the day or winding down after hours on the run. Surround yourself with colors, textures, materials, and accessories that make you feel comfortable, happy, and relaxed. Success comes from making choices that can be enjoyed day in and day out.

To create a mountain fresh bath for example, search out textured materials that look as though they have been harvested from the Rockies. If cool and sleek is a more suitable style, choose tile or stone finishes with a smooth, polished look.

If you are uncertain about which look is right for you and your family, take a tour through this gallery of ideas.

# Country Comfort

**Below:** Create the illusion of a big French sideboard by pulling the sink cabinet forward and installing flanking cabinets flush to the wall as shown. Cushioned benches flank the tub, enhancing the comfortable farmhouse flavor of the room.

To bring a fluent country French accent into a bathroom, begin with colors that could have been plucked from a rural European garden, such as these twilight blue ceramic tiles and flowering fabrics. Of course, no garden is complete without sunlight, so remember to plan for plenty of windows to bring in natural light: Include radiant yellow hues throughout the bath to keep the glow going around the clock. Infuse permanent sunshine using gilded frames and fixtures.

Whatever the color palette, the key to country decorating success hinges on balancing white-painted cabinetry and trim with wood flooring finished in a warm, rich stain for an aged look. Use the cabinets like pieces of French farmhouse furniture, adding such details as crown molding, doors with recessed panels or mullioned glass (ideal for displaying towels and accessories that enliven the room with more color), and lacy fretwork fascia that spans the gap between upper cabinets.

Creating country comfort in your bath can be as simple as including a few pieces of fine furniture. In the room above, the fixtures are purposefully arranged to make way for an upholstered chair. Even in a small bath, just one comfortable piece of furniture conveys the country feel.

Nostalgic accents make a room seem even cozier, so look to vintage-style materials and accessories to infuse warmth, such as the wide-plank salvaged pine floor and classic rug used here.

**Above: Provide plenty of storage and old-fashioned style using an antique armoire that's painted white, like this one. Complete the look with white-painted beaded board on the walls and tub surround.**

**Left: Another path to comfort: keep clutter under control. Here, dual vanities, divided by a lower makeup counter, work with two medicine cabinets and multiple drawers for easy organization.**

## DESIGNER TIP

**Bring living room comfort into your bathroom by adding rich, colorful fabrics. Upholstered chairs add enveloping warmth to the bath *above*. Padded window seats, throw pillows, and flowing fabric valances soften the bath *opposite*.**

No wasted space under these eaves: Stock cabinetry creates a built-in dressing table that's as pretty as it is practical.

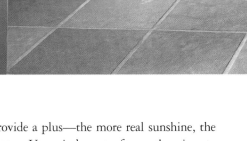

# Tropical Paradise

Setting sail for your own island oasis can be as easy as opening a can of paint. To create an illusionary island oasis, choose vibrant colors such as those commonly found in Caribbean resorts—warm sunny yellows and soothing sea blues. For added flavor, dot in the vibrant hues from tropical fruit—such as papaya pink and kiwi green.

Trim and other accents in white teamed with generous doses of sunlight are essential ingredients as well. Banks of windows always provide a plus—the more real sunshine, the better. Use windows to frame the view to emphasize the connection to the outdoors.

Feel free to creatively mix materials. Exotic getaways frequently blend textures and shapes. In this bath, the architect mixed matte slate floors and glossy Italian ceramic tiles with deep wooden moldings, a tongue-and-groove ceiling, and smooth, shapely pedestal sinks.

**Left:** Create a scene. Glaze-muted mustard yellow walls infuse this bath with golden tropical sunshine. Hand-painted dragonflies fluttering around intricate iron sconces add whimsy. Wooden pedestals, routed to match the sink's pedestal bases, raise the sinks to a height more comfortable for most users.

**Below:** Style is in the details. The slate floor picks up the greens introduced by the ceramic tiles on the tub surround. Golden accents add elegance.

## DESIGNER TIP

Think beyond the standard six sides of a box for determining a bath's shape:
• L-shape layouts, although uncommon, offer privacy and personal space for two people.
• A raised ceiling draws attention upward and adds volume, creating a sense of spaciousness.
• Floors needn't be one level. Elevated tubs and pedestal sinks accommodate users of different heights and visually break up the view.

White-washed woods, neutral floor tiles, and tempered glass walls focus attention on the blue and white tiled walls.

# Traditional Elegance

For centuries, blue and white delftware has captured decorators' fancy and remained a popular vintage collectible and decorating theme even today. If that's your passion, bring it into the bathroom, surrounding yourself with the things you love.

Create your own special look using today's enormous range of hand-painted tiles. Or create a one-of-a-kind pattern using varying solid colors and relief tiles from off-the-shelf sources.

Choose cabinetry that plays up the feeling formed by the tile. Enhancing the vintage, elegant designs in this bath is cabinetry with a whitewashed finish that keeps it from appearing brand new. Big 12x12-inch floor tiles repeat the tones of the cabinetry and continue into the shower, providing a subtle stage that allows the delft elements to provide the drama.

## COURTYARD CONNECTION

Any bathroom can benefit from a true connection to the outdoors. This bathroom is linked to the backyard with pretty French doors, which also bring in abundant sunlight during the day. Keep your outdoor connection private with a courtyard created from wood fencing, brick or stone walls, or a hedge of bushes. Use brick, stone, or stamped and colored concrete to form an elegant patio. Finish the mini-oasis with a comfortable chaise where you can kick back and wind down after a hot, relaxing shower. For more indoor-outdoor connection ideas, see pages 46–47.

In creating a classical setting, choose accessories to enhance the theme. In this bathroom, blue and white trimmings—such as the flowerpots and vases, and a tissue holder—team up with towels and fabrics in the same palette to sprinkle the colors throughout the bath.

Left: Identical wall-hung sconces add a touch of elegance to both of the bath's vanity areas. The stool features a needlepoint seat in blue and white.

Below: A spray of blue and white butterflies will forever flutter in this pretty sink basin. Brushed nickel faucets and handles convey a vintage look.

# European Flavor

If you long to create a bathroom that looks as though it hasn't changed for decades, glean the great ideas offered by this old world space. To truly maintain the integrity of days gone by, don't allow any contemporary elements into the room—not even recessed lighting. For example, if you're lucky enough to have windows, consider adding diamond-shape grilles to instantly "age" even the newest fenestrations. Paint the grilles silver, and rub black glaze on and off the wood slats to mimic a leaded-glass window. Another key to creating this traditional style is the use of ceramic tiles on the bathroom walls.

For this room, a textural combination of mossy green relief tiles and grids of nine tiny marble mosaics amid creamy field tiles add interest as well as European appeal. Bullnose tiles across the top of a partially tiled wall form a wainscoting effect around the room. Tiling around the bathtub—the only truly vintage element brought into this room—extends to the ceiling to accommodate a shower. As an elegant finish, limestone surfaces the floor and extends to the long white vanity as a countertop.

Why reserve your most beautiful things for your home's more public spaces? Many designers today decorate bathrooms as they

**Below left: Everything in the bath is brand new, except the vintage tub. Standing in for a ho-hum shower curtain is an etched-glass door that swings open. On the backsplash, grids of green marble mosaics punctuate cream color tiles. Above them, green relief tiles are topped by bullnose tiles.**
**Below right: Recessed leaded-glass windows influenced the design for this bath, then became the functional focal point by offering ledges for plants and accessories. On the floor, marble mosaics form a border around limestone squares set on the diagonal.**

Left: A white-painted chair rail provides the dividing detail for the dramatic painted treatment on the walls. Crown molding at the ceiling amplifies the room's prominence. A wrought-iron chandelier reinforces the fact that no bath has to be ordinary.

## ART IN THE BATH

Reveal your artistic sensibilities in creating a new bathroom. These spaces demonstrate two approaches. In the old world bathroom, *opposite*, artwork over the tub is a composite of green square and cream relief tiles set on the diagonal with a frame of the same bullnose tiles used elsewhere. Completing the rich red bathroom, *left*, are an assortment of framed prints that help infuse the space with a luxurious atmosphere.

would the living room or study. Even the most petite powder room can prove that some of the best surprises really do come inside small packages.

Paying attention to every detail is especially important in a small space because every item is readily noticeable. Rather than take the approach that this is a hopelessly small utilitarian room, for example, treat a tiny bath or powder room to features that bring in the elegance of an English library. To establish the look, finish three walls in a plush, two-prong paint treatment. Above the chair rail, rag on ruby-color paints and glazes;

below the molding, drag subtle shades of taupe paint with a paint comb to create a striated design. Of course, every library needs at least one bookcase. Include one to span the space between the top of the toilet tank and the ceiling.

For more drama, add an arched fascia board and fluted pilasters. Here, a bright band of red tiles underscores this bookcase, which displays a few books and decorative items. For the final detail, search flea markets and antiques stores for a fitting period-look light fixture.

# Ahhh Spa

**Above: By suspending a vanity on the wall, it appears to float—an uncluttered look that's easy on the eyes. When choosing an above-the-counter sink, such as this 8-inch-deep granite bowl, keep in mind that you may need to install a slightly lower countertop for comfort.**

Here's the ticket to launching your resort-inspired bath: Borrow beautiful materials from nature. A sleek maple vanity proves that clean lines don't have to be clinical with a rich, honey-tone wood. For a touch of elegance, add a silky, travertine countertop. To create a grooming area that's easy on the eyes, wrap the walls above the vanity in mirrors augmented with plenty of lighting. Tube lights, such as the ones pictured here, come in both incandescent and color-corrected fluorescent to cast a favorable glow. Finally, add an above-the-counter granite vessel sink that will remind you of splashing in a clear mountain stream—a sure-fire way to wash stresses away.

For inspiration in creating a spa-style bathroom, take a walk along the beach and notice how such elements as sand, bleached shells, and water soothe the soul. That sense of tranquility can be translated to the bathroom decor. Like cool, clear water, an aqua-colored glass countertop in this bathroom forms an undulating wave around the sink basin.

Sandblasted glass tiles, visible on the wall beneath the countertop in the bath pictured, are reminiscent of a fog rolling in across the water.

Use contrast to accent the spa-like choices. As a clean counterpoint to the ocean hues in this bath, the designer chose a bright white sink, vanity base, and wide wood trim. Gleaming chrome fittings finish the vanity area with the same glint sunshine gives to ocean waves on sunny days.

Left: Change the ambience in a bath from blah to spa simply by lighting aromatic candles and playing favorite mood music. Pamper yourself with fragrant bath oils, lotions, scented soaps, and shampoos and you'll leave the grooming room with a whole new attitude.

Curving lines are more appealing than straight ones, but a vanity shape like this is also practical. It narrows to ease the transition between spaces.

## A SOFT TOUCH

Include a stack of extra-thick white towels that feel good on the skin to complete the ambience of the spa-style bath. Add a heated bar to hang them on and you'll always have a toasty towel ready when you step out of the tub or shower. Hang a monogrammed terry robe on a nearby bath hook to complete your better-than-any-day-spa cover-up.

# Timeless Treasure

Opposites attract, and the idea is truer when it's expressed in black and white. One of the best aspects of this crisp combination is its ability to blend contemporary and vintage designs, an especially favorable approach when updating a bath in an old house.

To blend old and new, try a vintage flooring design of white ceramic tile punctuated with black tiles. Tuck a purely contemporary in-floor heating system below the tile to ensure toasty toes whenever you step out of the tub or shower.

Wallpaper offers readily changeable opportunities; use it to direct the style leanings toward old or new. Black-and-white stripe wallcovering lends bold, graphic appeal that's timeless. For a more traditional look, try toile. For a contemporary feel, consider a geometric print.

On a wall opposite a window, a long mirror will reflect the outdoor view and make the room seem larger than its dimensions. A glass enclosure for an extra-large shower can also help visually expand the space. Add muscle-massaging showerheads to bring a luxurious grand finale to any bath.

**Left:** By adding tiles, a raised threshold, and glass doors, you can cordon off one entire end of a bathroom to create an especially roomy shower. **Below:** Cap a long vanity with a lower table to gain the perfect spot for hair styling or applying cosmetics.

To play up the vintage roots of true Craftsman style, fashion vanities from marble to mimic the look of charming old laundry sinks, but mount them on stylish mahogany legs for open-air appeal.

# Art of the Craft

With today's always-on-the-run schedules, some people crave simplicity wherever they can find it. That may be why the clean lines of Craftsman styling make an especially pleasing choice for master-suite retreats. Concentrating a bathroom design around grid designs and wide, flat bands of mahogany around windows, mirrors, and the tub surround can capture the look. For a cool, restful balance to these warm tones, consider creamy marble flooring.

Corner windows placed high create the ideal spot for an oversize whirlpool tub tucked into the corner. The outdoor view and doses of sun or moonlight are daily bonuses. If your bathroom space allows, include a roomy walk-in shower for enjoying a post-workout steam or an invigorating spray whether it's time to start or finish the day.

At the other end of the spectrum is the joyous visual cacophony of the abstract artistic design that attracts a different crowd. Even a petite bathroom can feature energizing artistic power. Use the patterns of a favored piece of artwork and interpret the design on the walls either in paint or tile mosaic. Simply project the desired image on the wall and trace with pencil. Then fill in lines with paint or broken tiles. Feel free to alter colors as desired to make it a personal expression of style. In this bathroom, for example, pieces of marble and granite form a colorful version of Picasso's black and white masterpiece, *Guernica*. Divide a small bath into sections to form a separate compartment for the shower or toilet, and include a cutout area within the wall to prevent the spaces from feeling too cramped. Add a shelf to the cutout to display more artwork.

**Far left: To enjoy the benefit of a clutter-free environment, design a tall mahogany cabinet to stand beside the vanity.** Above: **Picasso loved to skew perspective. The sink, bird's eye-maple cabinet, and mirror are placed at intriguing angles within the niche.** Left: **Enlivening the shower is a scene of a woman fleeing a fire, interpreted from the Picasso masterpiece** *Guernica*—**a painting about the bombing of a Spanish village. In this tiled version, however, every touch of the faucet douses the flames.**

# Form Meets Function

Creating a bath design to meet the functional and aesthetic needs of two or more people is the toughest test—and most common situation. The lessons for success start here.

**Right:** The homeowners opted for minimal window treatments and bright white tiles in the steam shower to keep the bathing area light and the views as pristine as possible. Tucked in a corner, the green checked upholstery of the overstuffed chair complements the green in the marble countertops and adds another touch of color to the bath.

Establishing clear goals for a new bath is the key to its success. Set primary goals by determining how each person will use the space. The more precise the goals, the more likely the final design will meet expectations. Start by taking detailed stock of the present bathroom situation. Consider everything from materials to the fundamental issues such as layout and fixture location. Perhaps simply installing new flooring, wall coverings, countertops, cabinetry, or fixtures will solve the problems. Or maybe just rearranging the bath's layout so that it will better meet the needs of its primary users will do the job.

If those options don't solve the dilemmas, more work—adding on to the existing bath or creating an entirely new bath—may be required. Whatever your needs, balance them against the budgetary bottom line. Later in this book you'll get a financial picture of a bath remodeling. For now, just remember to keep your form and function planning decisions in touch with your financial realities.

# Family Revelry: Jack and Jill Plans

Is more than one family member slated to use your new bath? You may want to consider a Jack and Jill-style floor plan. Divided into three separate rooms, these baths feature two separate vanity rooms with a shared tub/shower and toilet area.

This style is particularly useful for baths shared by siblings. Each sibling walks from his or her own bedroom into his or her own private vanity room.

Here a ceramic tile mirror and feminine wall covering accent the girl's area, while a masculine striped paper and a metal mirror frame add personality to the boy's room.

## Corner Plans

The Jack and Jill configuration *near right* works well in attic installations if you need to skirt a low ceiling. The version *far right* offers an easy way to work around an existing closet, half-bath, or utility space.

## Square Plans

If you have a square area of remodeling space available, consider installing a bath configured like the one *near right.* The plan works well for same-sex siblings and features a shared double vanity area and a linen closet. The *far right* plan provides each child with a separate sink area, sharing only toilet and tub.

## Rectangular Plans

Rectangular plans work well in homes where the bedrooms are located on the same side of a hallway. The example *near right* provides a solution for working around a staircase. The bath *far right* was created by annexing a 3-foot-wide section of space from two adjoining bedrooms.

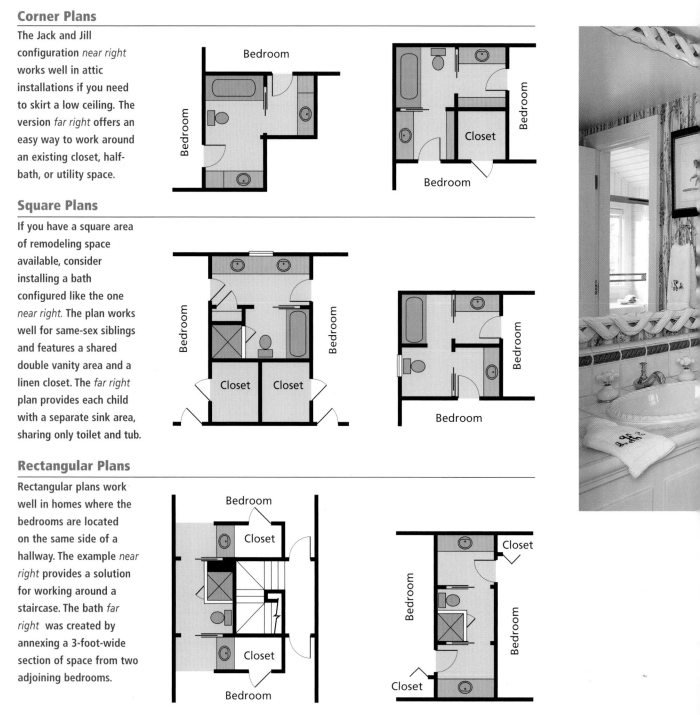

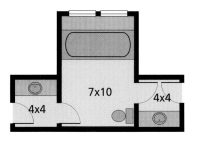

From private vanity areas, each sibling can enter the gender-neutral, centrally located foot tub and shower area. For added convenience, incorporate a movable showerhead to fit the varying heights of different users.

If space is too tight for separate vanity rooms for each child, consider installing a vanity area in each bedroom, and take the pressure off sharing a centrally located bath.

**Below left and right:** Although cabinetry and fixtures are identical, different decorating details in the vanity rooms give a sense of individuality to each area.

**Left:** In the shared tub/shower and toilet area, the look is gender neutral. Beaded-board wainscoting adds architectural interest. A deep tile ledge adjacent to the tub offers ample storage for each teen's bath toiletries.

Jack and Jill schemes are not limited to addressing the needs of siblings. Baths shared by parents and siblings or guests and family members can achieve a level of privacy for grooming while sharing a common bathing space.

Here, for example, a family member's bedroom and the guest bedroom share the same shower, tub, and toilet space. The vanity is used by a young girl and is decorated in colors and fabrics to match her adjoining bedroom. Additional pink and yellow accents in her vanity area provide a decorative tie to the shared tub area. The shared area of the bathroom displays colors and fabrics from both the guest bedroom and the little girl's room.

These plans also work for master baths. In a master bath, separate entrances from the same bedroom lead to separate vanity and dressing areas, and the shower and tub space is located in the middle.

**Above and right: Typically, the vanity rooms in Jack and Jill baths use matching countertops and faucets but the decor is decidedly different in each. The vanity** *above* **was decorated with guest use in mind while the one at** *right* **suits a young girl. Opposite: The shower area color scheme mixes colors and fabrics from the individual vanity areas.**

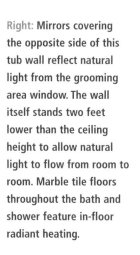

# Room for Two: Compartmentalization

Compartmentalizing a master bath enables spouses to share the bathroom while offering privacy to each. In these bath plans, separate compartments house the toilet (and sometimes include a bidet and a shower too).

This type of plan, however, can be a space-grabber. Here, the wall to an underutilized guest bedroom that adjoined the master bedroom was removed. Divided into four rectangular-shaped areas, the nearly square bath plan features a C-shape grooming area with wraparound vanities and a sep-

arate makeup counter. Sinks are angled in opposite corners of the grooming space. A partial wall between the tub and vanity area provides privacy without blocking light. Opposite the tub, a walk-in shower allows enough room for two, eliminating any wait. Corner benches offer sit-down comfort and toiletry storage. A separate private compartment houses a toilet and bidet.

If you don't want to relinquish an entire bedroom to create an elaborate compartmentalized bath plan, you may need to add on. Another option is to scale back plans. Here

14x15

are less costly solutions that create compartments in a smaller space:

• In a standard-size 5x8-foot bathroom, where the toilet and shower sit just beyond the vanity cabinet, shorten the vanity by a few inches. Then fill in the newly created space with a wall and sliding pocket door to separate the tub and toilet from the vanity.

• Installing a half-wall instead of a full wall isn't as private but saves costs.

• Prefer something even simpler? Set up a folding privacy screen to keep the commode out of view from the other areas of the bath.

**Above: Because this C-shape vanity area is fairly compact, the designer/builder maintained adequate floor space by creating counters just 18 inches deep. Left: In the custom shower, two showerheads are fitted on opposing walls. A third, extra-large showerhead is mounted overhead.**

# Space-Expanding Style

Below right: **Padded walls
provide sound insulation
for this little bath and
prevent the small space
from becoming an echo
chamber. The room's
yellow, blue, and white
color scheme, along with a
white beaded-board
covered ceiling, creates a
lighthearted ambience.
Rounded trim tiles
prevent items from rolling
off the countertop.**
Below: **A tiled half-wall
surrounds the sink and
protects the wall from
sink spatters. Yellow and
white checkerboard floor
tiles are laid on the
diagonal to create the
illusion of greater width.**

There are many other ways to make your present bath space look, feel, and live larger. To increase floor space, consider replacing a standard-size vanity with a 10-inch-deep cabinet like the one shown below. This custom-made, built-in, tile-covered cabinet contains linen storage behind inset wooden doors. To increase storage near a pedestal sink, add a wall-hung medicine cabinet in place of a standard vanity mirror, then add a 8-inch-wide ledge behind the sink to provide space for curling irons, makeup, and other toiletries.

If your bath is located on an exterior wall, add or increase windows. Windows let in natural light, fresh air, and scenic views while preventing small bath spaces from feeling cramped and claustrophobic.

If you can't squeeze enough space out of the existing bath and adding on is out of the question, look for a more creative solution using space near the bath. Using the landing at the top of the stairs for a furniture-style vanity was the solution in this tiny two-story home, *opposite*. Two sinks, a shower, and a toilet wouldn't fit in one place in the undereaves space, so eaved space on one side of the stair holds a roomy shower, toilet, and pedestal sink, while eaved space on the opposite side of the stair holds a second sink fitted into a standard dresser, built-in storage, a dressing area, and a closet.

**Left:** Installing a sink in an a dresser alleviates the need for sharing the new bath's small pedestal sink and provides more counter space. Drawers and shelves in the nearby knee wall provide storage for clothing and linens.
**Below:** A tub would have been a too-tight squeeze. The solution was opting for a roomy shower instead. A new skylight above the shower provides plenty of headroom.

## DESIGNER TIP

To create a sink vanity from a standard dresser, have a cabinetmaker cut a hole in the top of a dresser to fit a drop-in-style sink, and then coat the remaining wooden surface with polyurethane to protect it from water and spills. A combination sink and dresser can double as a makeup center. If space permits, add a matching chest of drawers for more storage.

Installing a self-rimmed
bowl into a dining room
sideboard creates a
one-of-a-kind vanity that
is as attractive
as it is functional.

# Freestanding Furniture

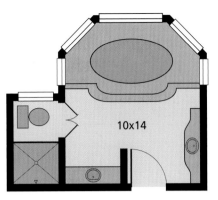

If you love the look of fine furniture and like the idea of converting a bedroom dresser into a vanity base, consider converting a sideboard or dining hutch into a vanity. The mahogany Sheraton sideboard, *opposite,* once stood in the dining room. An interior designer suggested using the piece to create a feminine bath vanity. A similar, but more masculine piece—a mahogany chest with clean lines and nearly identical hardware—was turned into a second vanity.

Unite distinctly different vanities by visually connecting them with matching or complementary faucets and sinks. Likewise, mount similar mirrors and sconces above each vanity. Don't be afraid to vary vanity heights to fit the individual needs of each user; 36-inch-high vanities are more comfortable for people over 5 feet, 8 inches tall while 30-inch-high vanities are more comfortable for people of smaller stature.

Fit vanities on opposite or perpendicular walls to help solve traffic-flow problems that can occur when two people must share the space at the same time.

Private shower and toilet areas on inside walls can feel dark and closed off. To prevent this, consider separating the area with glass-paneled doors that have been covered with semi-sheer or lace curtain panels, such as the doors below. The panels let in the light, yet still provide adequate privacy.

10x14

Above: **Think about the traffic flow. Narrow French doors separate the shower and toilet area from the main bath; the narrow doors fit the space without blocking the area in front of the sink.**
Left: **To take advantage of all the available storage space, the bottom center drawer is customized to open and close around plumbing pipes.**

## THE RIGHT LIGHT

• If possible, install vanity lighting—the kind of light needed for shaving or applying makeup—at eye level on both sides of the mirror. Using just overhead lighting creates less-than-flattering shadows.

• If overhead lights are the only option, choose a white countertop so that the upward light reflection will reduce the shadowing. For accurate skin coloring, choose incandescent bulbs; avoid bulbs that cast a golden glow.

• Illuminate other areas in the bath with recessed or track lighting, which are unobtrusive yet highly functional.

• Provide separate controls for recessed lighting and vanity lighting, and give each a dimmer switch so that you can control the mood, whether for a relaxing soak in the tub or for scrubbing away dirt after a busy day.

# Privacy Preferred

If you've never really savored the thought of sharing bath space, consider building two smaller baths in the same amount of space normally occupied by a single bath.

Incorporating built-in cabinets and paying special attention to placing plumbing fixtures make this type of design successful and keep it from feeling like two teeny-tiny bathrooms placed back-to-back.

The interior designer on this project used similar hues—ivory-tone wallpaper, for example—to tie the spaces to each other and to the adjoining bedroom, then varied the decor to make each bath fit the personality of the user. Similarly styled vanity hutches tie the spaces together but the look of each is distinctly different. The hutches are also great organizers since neatness is a crucial issue in small spaces such as this. Mirrors and light fixtures are incorporated in the cabinetry and electrical sockets for hair dryers, shavers, and curling irons are behind hutch doors.

Closet

Her Bath

Closet

His Bath

Master Bedroom

**Abundant traditional details, like the arched alcove above the tub in her bath,** *opposite,* **and ceiling moldings and furniture-style built-ins in both rooms,** *below* **and** *right,* **make these separate his-and-her baths feel more inviting than utilitarian.**

# Dressing Room

Space planning is often the toughest part of planning a bath project. Existing plumbing lines, chimney flues, and other permanent features of a home may require placing a new bath in an unconventional location or irregular-shape space, or inhibit your plans for updating an existing bath. Fitting in the necessities is difficult enough, much less finding room for the amenities.

Creative thinking about space allows you to add the right kinds of spaces. A dressing room, for example, may seem an amenity. But if fitting in the bathroom basics, adequate closet and dresser space, as well as having sufficient room to get ready to face the day are on the list, including a dressing room may be the answer.

Part bath, part bedroom, a dressing room takes the space squeeze off two rooms.

**Below right:** A pocket door located between two floor-to-ceiling storage cabinets separates the bathing area of the bath from this dressing area.
**Center:** Because the entrance to the suite is only 8 feet wide, the designer installed mirrors on both sides: one above the double vanity and another above the built-in dressers. An abundance of storage in the dressing room eliminates the need for dressers in the adjoining bedroom.

In this two-story tract home, the owners knew the only logical place to add a master suite addition was over the garage. Due to the location of the eaves and existing plumbing lines, the new master bath had to serve as the passageway to the bedroom. Making part of the space look more like a hallway and less like a bathroom was a difficult objective.

The solution was dividing the space into a bathroom and a dressing area. The dressing area measures 8 feet wide by 17 feet long, one long wall with a limestone-topped double vanity and two floor-to-ceiling storage cabinets for linen and clothing storage. At the other long side of the dressing area are two built-in dressers and two more floor-to-ceiling storage cabinets.

This arrangement allows for unplanned bonuses: A large skylight welcomes the sun, and the storage keeps the clothing and linen clutter out of the bedroom.

Left: Sharing materials helps tie spaces together. The tub surround is made from the same French limestone as the countertops in the dressing area. To maximize the view and privacy, a cellular shade is tucked behind the cherry window frame.

Above: Interior glass-block windows and a crisp white decorating scheme brighten this indoor/outdoor space even further. Right: A tempered glass door dresses the steam shower. The shower is also equipped with a bench for spa appeal.

# Outdoor Connection

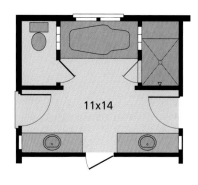

11x14

Although baths are often on outside walls, rarely is that proximity to the outdoors used to advantage. Bath layouts that provide direct access to a pool, lake, outdoor hot tub, or garden can make a home feel more like a unique, luxurious retreat and less like every other house in the neighborhood.

Consider the advantages a bathroom that opens to the outdoors can give your home: Doors and windows bring in fresh air and sunlight, frame views, and provide a spot for quick cleanup after gardening, swimming, or sunbathing. All this openness can create privacy issues, but those can be readily addressed. Look for window treatments that cover windows and doors when needed but can be moved out of the way to allow in natural light or moonlit views when desired.

Think of ease too. Motorized shades move up and down with the touch of a button. Or, install shades or plantation shutters that cover cover the lower portion of the window for privacy, leaving the upper reaches uncovered for light and views. To get the light deep in the room, use glass block for interior window spaces.

Take advantage of the landscape for privacy. Tall pines prevent anyone from seeing into this bathroom; tall fences or thick hedges can do the same for first-floor baths.

**Left:** A row of black and white, tumbled-marble tiles accentuates the white countertop, tiled half-wall, and tub surround. To keep material costs within budget, the remaining white bath tiles are ceramic that has been made to resemble marble. Sleek nickel-finish pulls adorn the bath's separate-but-equal vanities.

Right: A partial wall keeps the commode out of the sight lines of the adjoining entry hall. A hammered-chrome sink with its unique stair-step shape inspired the dividing wall's stair-step design. Metallic fabric paints, splashed on in a carefree pattern, adorn the walls.

# Perfect Powder Rooms

Treat your guests like royalty by adding a touch of style to the powder room. Whether glitz hits the spot, *above*, or country fits the bill, *opposite*, little extras make a big difference. If your choices seem extravagant, remember that you only need a little bit of anything to fill a powder room.

Shaped sinks with cabinets that angle back are not only elegant, but they also use less precious floor space than standard vanity cabinets. A pedestal sink is a good choice to keep the space open.

Powder rooms are often on high-traffic hallways; that can mean very little privacy and a lot of public inspection from people walking past. The simple amenities of wall and window coverings create a more pleasing view for passersby.

Pocket doors solve the problem of sufficient door swing, and every powder room door deserves a good lock. A partial wall keeps the commode out of view and ensures modesty. Or add a dressing screen to partition the room.

Sometimes the children's bath is the ersatz powder room for guests. If that's the case, consider giving the children an adjacent, separate, vanity area so guests won't have to work around a teen's abundant grooming supplies or wade through a toddler's splish-splash from hand washing.

Budget for good lighting. Not only will your guests appreciate the flattering glow, family members ducking in for a quick primp will like it as well. Wall sconces flanking a mirror convey a cozy, room-like feel—much better than the harsh shadows cast by a standard-issue ceiling fixture.

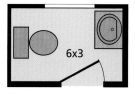

**Left: Old-fashioned wallpaper and a matching balloon shade combine with a sink pedestal made from a French harvest basket to create a vintage look in this tiny powder room.**

## MAKING THE MOST OF SMALL SPACES

Powder rooms aren't the only small bathrooms. Perfect placement is key when square footage is limited. This selection of floor plans for petite bathrooms shows how you can have everything in 75 square feet or less.

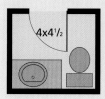

This half bath requires only 15 square feet of living space. It could easily fit in the space of a closet, mudroom, or laundry area.

Though it measures only 5x7 feet, this bathroom contains generous countertop space and base cabinet 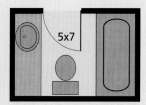 storage. It would work well for a teen who has lots of grooming supplies.

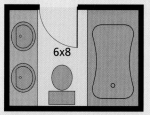 As this floor plan demonstrates, with careful planning, you can fit stylish fixtures into a modestly sized space. Occupying only 48 square feet, the bath contains a generous-size tub and two sinks.

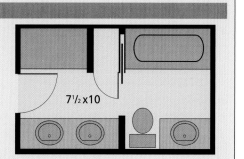

This compartmentalized bath is designed to meet the needs of an entire family.

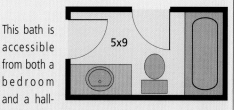

This bath is accessible from both a bedroom and a hallway. To create more clear walkway space, replace the swinging door near the toilet with a pocket door.

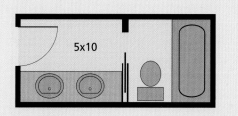

Designed for two people to use simultaneously, this bath has an interior pocket door to create privacy within a limited amount of space. Adding a second pocket door to the wall across from the sinks could create access to another bedroom or hallway.

# Universal Design

If you're redoing a bath in a house you plan to stay in for many years, consider incorporating barrier-free elements. Ingenious products and well-thought-out plans make today's accessible baths as visually appealing as any other. Even if you never require the added accessibility yourself, a friend or family member who may will appreciate your forethought. Consider installing some of these features into the bath when you build or remodel.

This bath, *right,* features a sink vanity with 30 inches of clear knee space so a wheelchair can be pulled in close. Textured ceramic tile floors help prevent falls. A pull-down shower seat flips up and out of the way when not in use.

A short wall attractively delineates the extra-wide, thresholdless shower, *opposite,* from the toilet; a similar wall separates the vanity area from the shower. A slope toward the shower drain in the tiled floor takes care of runoff. The limestone-look tiles are actually made from a composite material that provides more give than stone while offering equally easy wheeling. The low vanity with semi-encased sink, protected plumbing, and

**Right: Faucet and fixtures were chosen for both appearance and ease of operation. For safety purposes, always install grab bars into wall studs for maximum support.**

## PLAY IT SAFE!

A small investment in bath safety can help keep your family out of harm's way.

• To prevent electrocution, make sure all electrical outlets are equipped with ground fault circuit interrupters.

• To prevent drowning, never leave a small child unattended in the bathtub. Keep washcloths and toys at tubside so you won't be tempted to walk away for any reason. Install a childproof latch on the toilet lid.

• To prevent scalding, lower the water heater temperature to 120 degrees. As an added precaution, install pressure-balanced faucets.

• To help prevent cuts and bruises, add a cushion to the tub spout. (Waterproof cushions in various shapes are readily available at many bath and hardware centers.) If possible, round countertop and cabinetry corners. Choose rugs with nonskid backing, and install rubber footpads on all step stools and vanity chairs to prevent them from slipping when in use.

• Finally, if you EVER have young children in your house, install childproof locks on all cabinets.

## ACCESSIBLE BATHS

For more information on accessible baths, including proper dimensions and additional safety precautions, see Barrier-Free Baths on pages 114–115.

lack of undercabinets makes it easy and comfortable to pull up a wheelchair.

### Accessorize for safety

Grab bars installed throughout the bath provide stability to all users, and when not in use, they can double as towel bars. Lever-handled door handles and faucet controls, such as the ones shown in both of these featured baths, are easier to operate by anyone with limited mobility. Antiscald faucets reduce scalding risks for both children and adults. Adjustable handheld showerheads are especially convenient in homes occupied by people with extreme variations in height.

Above: For easy access, the shower stall has no curb and is wide enough for a complete wheelchair turnaround. The low bench in the shower provides accessible storage and can be used to accommodate transfers from the chair.

# Dreams to Reality

After functional needs are met, it's time to determine the best way to transform a bath vision into an affordable reality.

Right: **You may be able to give your bath a new look with affordable fixes. Rather than gut the guest bathroom in this '20s-era house, the owner saved money by reglazing the bathtub and installing new fixtures. Inexpensive bifold doors conceal the tub and provide bathing privacy. Painting the existing wood vanity black adds drama to the sink. Wallpaper depicting maps of Paris adds elegance to the walls.**

Bathroom remodeling projects fall into at least one of five categories. At the lowest cost and least complicated end of the spectrum is the *facelift,* which involves making cosmetic changes (such as resurfacing walls or floors or replacing fixtures) to an existing bathroom. Somewhat more involved and costly is *renovation,* which encompasses changing the layout, enlarging or replacing windows, and making structural changes short of expansion. Next comes *expanding* an existing bathroom into adjacent space—a closet, hallway, or bedroom, for example.

If you need more bathrooms, your options include *converting* existing square footage to bathroom use and—at the top end of the cost and complexity scale—*building* an addition.

It's rare that a project falls neatly into just one of these categories; most are a blend. This chapter explores a full range of options to help you determine what strategy will best meet your bath remodeling goals.

# Same Space Facelift

A bath that works well but looks dated or bland can benefit from an infusion of style from a facelift. Facelifts include all nonstructural, cosmetic changes, such as repainting or papering the walls, resurfacing walls or tub surrounds, and/or replacing fixtures, flooring, and countertops.

Just some fresh paint, a few rolls of wallpaper, and new hardware can work miracles, transforming a bland space to a beautiful room. An interior designer revamped this bath by covering the dark surfaces with lighter shades and then reworking the existing storage to increase its efficiency.

Wide neutral-stripe paper replaced dark burgundy and navy florals. A border of tumbled marble in soft creams keeps the soft neutral look going. Existing floor and wall tiles were refreshed with a restorative acid wash. The existing dark-stained vanity cabinet was covered with a warm white, weathered-looking paint.

Get more storage and function from existing cabinets by making their interior

**Below: A coat of white paint and new flower-shaped iron drawer pulls update an existing vanity cabinet. Glossy Italian marble replaces the vanity's original countertop.**

Above: The custom-made cabinet fits in a once-empty spot by the tub. The fronts of the top four drawers form a cabinet door; the bottom drawers remain operable. Left: The cleverly hinged shower curtain provides privacy for the tub or the shower. Below left: This storage cabinet was revamped to organize bottles, jars, and tubes instead of linens.

design match individual storage needs. The shallow closet, *left,* once served as barely functional linen storage. The cabinet interior was reworked so that the closet would serve better as a medicine chest. A shallow mirror on the door makes the vanity area appear more spacious and enables the homeowners to get a floor-to-ceiling glimpse of their attire.

If necessary, add freestanding furniture to supplement storage. The linen storage chest, *above right,* was made to fit into the previously unused space adjacent to the tub.

**Right:** Installing white beaded-board paneling and painting the walls sunflower yellow changed the character of this once dark bath from gloomy to sunny. A white sink and white marble countertop reflect light from the vanity area's fixtures, increasing illumination for both shaving and applying makeup.

## Work your colors

Neutrals create a soothing ambience and visually expand a room's dimensions; bright colors offer warmer, lighthearted looks. Many rooms contain both, and the color that dominates sets the tone.

The bathroom of this Portland, Oregon, home transformed from dull to cheery with a facelift. Sunflower yellow paint replaces brown plaid wallpaper. A new white toilet sits where a dated, dark brown one once did. A white sink and marble countertop replace a glazed pottery sink and laminate counters.

For additional interest, double up on wall treatments. Here, narrow plank beaded paneling was installed on the lower half of the walls, using the windowsill as the dividing line. Be sure to coat wooden paneling with scrubbable paint. This paneling was covered with an easy-to clean oil base paint that also holds up well in a bath's humid conditions.

Downplay utility with decoration. In this bath, brass cabinet pulls and brass-and-porcelain faucets add shine; a pretty blue plate holds guest soaps.

## VISUALLY EXPAND YOUR SPACE

Here are a few simple changes that can make a diminutive bath feel and live larger:

• **Add light.** Eliminate shadowy corners by installing an overhead fixture, downlights, or wall sconces. To increase natural light, install a skylight or simply replace an existing bath window with a larger one. Use mirrors to reflect the light you do have and to create an appearance of more square footage.

• **Downsize.** Trade larger fixtures for smaller ones. In this bath, *left*, a sink and base cabinets were replaced with a sleek pedestal and a recessed medicine cabinet. Replace a full-size tub with a roomy, yet smaller shower.

• **Tone it down.** Whites, pastels, and neutrals reflect light and make a small area feel larger. Darker shades absorb light and make a room feel smaller. Paint background elements, such as woodwork, trim, and doors, white or in the same hue as the walls to diminish their impact. Use a light color of paint on the walls and a lighter color on the ceiling to draw the eye upward.

• **Streamline.** Clutter takes up precious space and makes a tiny room look overly full. Pare countertop objects to the minimum and store the rest. Recess shelves into the stud space to create sight lines with a minimum of interruptions. If your bathroom has a shower, clear glass doors will stretch sight lines, while frosted glass creates a visual wall.

Left: **A deep oval sink, marble countertop, and beaded paneling backsplash transport this bath back to the 1920s, the era in which the home was built. Even the porcelain rheostat harkens to an earlier era.**

# Same Space Renovate

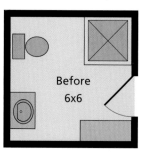

Before
6x6

After
6x6

Renovation goes beyond cosmetic changes to encompass replacing fixtures, changing the layout, adding lighting, enlarging or replacing windows, and making any structural changes short of expansion. Although this remodeling option is typically more costly than a facelift, it can dramatically change the functionality of your bath, possibly making it feel bigger and fit better without adding on.

In this tiny 6x6-foot bath renovation, *below,* the architect had the space gutted and then had the fixtures rearranged to make it fit the needs of growing teenagers now and overnight guests later.

If your bath has a 2-foot-square shower that is barely big enough to turn around in, replace it with a wider model that has a corner opening. The new shower looks and feels larger and its new corner location prevents the shower and bath's entrance door from banging into each other. To provide space for toiletries, increase the vanity's width so that there is more storage space below and more counter space on top.

Make the bath as attractive and timeless as possible by choosing fixtures that will look good both now and years from now. A mahogany base cabinet has been topped with black marble. A marble chair rail, accented with ceramic rope trim, stands in

**Below:** The bath's new shower stall features a glass door and glass walls on two sides, making the room dimensions seem larger. The white fiberglass walls also provide a bright spot against the room's darker tones. Using a lighter shade of paint on the upper wall and painting the ceiling molding white draws the eye up and adds dimension.

Left: A wall-to-wall mirror and gleaming ceramic tiles prevent this closet-size bath from feeling claustrophobic. Pairing the toilet and sink on one wall provides more floor space. The painted wood and limestone tile frame adds an elegant touch to a basic mirror. The same limestone adds a decorative touch to the wall and visually ties the wall and the floor together.

as a backsplash above the sink. Black and white marble tiles add contrast and complete the look.

## Go with the flow

Even a simple change, such as hinging a door on the opposite side can make a big difference in bath function. Before the renovation, the bath door in the bath, *above,* swung into the toilet. Guests had to enter the bath, squeeze against the counter, and then shut the door. Although the door swing in this bath didn't change, a pedestal sink in place of the countertop and base cabinet increased floor space and eliminated the problem. The owner felt that giving up some underutilized storage for a more comfortable fixture arrangement was a more-than-fair trade.

Your bath will last for years when you choose surfaces that will stand up to the abuse and are of colors you can live with for a long time. Here, the owner loves bright colors, and blue is one color she says she'll likely never tire of, so she used it in a periwinkle shade in the half bath.

Use mirrors to make a small space seem larger. This bath uses a 5-foot-square mirror to cover the top half of one wall, preventing the 5x5-foot color intense room from feeling claustrophobic.

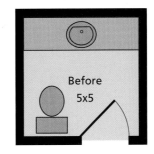

Before
5x5

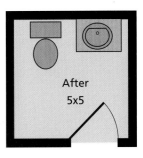

After
5x5

## Relocate

Renovating an existing bath may require removing or adding walls within the existing bath space. Sometimes the floorplan keeps a bath from functioning well. In this bathroom, the toilet sat in the middle of the room, directly across from a window. The shower and tub, too, were overexposed to the outside world.

To make the bath more functional, the troublesome window was eliminated. To compensate for the lost sunlight, the ceiling was vaulted and a skylight installed. This element provides much-needed natural light while preserving privacy. A new enclosed corner shower and separated toilet compartment also increase the room's privacy.

Once necessary floor plan changes are made, look to the bath's remaining free space for adding finer touches. Add a wide ledge to one end of the whirlpool tub for bath oils,

Across and in perfect viewing location from the tub, a rolltop cabinet hides a television set. The TV keeps the family up to date with morning news and encourages relaxation at the end of a long day. A shallow built-in cabinet adjacent to the TV houses smaller toiletry items.

Left: Separate vanities ease the morning rush. Small stainless-steel sinks increase counter space, providing additional spots for toiletries and whatnot. Below: The whirlpool tub provides the focal point of this bath, while the corner shower location offers a bit more privacy. Roomy enough for two people, the shower sports dual showerheads and a bench seat.

candles, and sponges. Fill remaining wall space with storage hutches. Add a tall cabinet, like the one in this bath, to house a television or a towel warming drawer. Warm tile or stone floors with radiant heat coils installed within the subflooring.

The importance of proper bath lighting almost can't be overstated. Here, uplighting washes the ceiling with light and halogen downlights provide proper illumination for grooming. Downlighting creates shadows, and the sidelighting eliminates those shadows.

# More space
## Expand

**Above:** The original 7x13-foot dimensions (bath and two closets) were set in brick: The load-bearing wall separating the bath and the new addition had to stay. The solution was to move the closet into the new space and transform the old closets into bath space. **Right:** To keep plumbing costs reasonable, the toilet did not move; walls and a door were added around it to create privacy.

Sometimes the amount of space in an existing bathroom is simply insufficient, and borrowing square footage from adjoining areas, such as a closet, hallway, or bedroom, is required. Annexing space from an adjoining room solves most problems caused by too-tight dimensions. If at all possible, look first to closets and other spaces that adjoin your bathroom's "plumbing wall"—the wall that already contains plumbing pipes. It's far less expensive to install fixtures when you can connect them to nearby plumbing lines. Likewise, non-load-bearing walls that have little or no utility lines are much easier and less costly to remove than load-bearing walls with utility lines.

Sandwiched between two closets, the once maze-like bath featured here was livable when just one person needed to get ready for work. But when the homeowner got married, he and his wife were bumping elbows in the bath every time they turned around. The bath's intrinsic layout problems could no longer be ignored. With no additional interior space available, they decided to add on, enclosing the space over the porch. It was a smart choice: If existing interior square footage can't be converted, porches and breezeways are the most cost-effective choices for gaining space.

Look at the combined spaces as a single new space, and make improvements within the allotted space with smart organization.

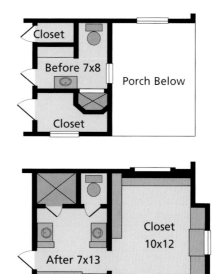

Closet

Before 7x8

Porch Below

Closet

Closet
10x12

After 7x13

Tuck built-in dressers close to the walls to maximize floor space. Use a window seat to provide a landing spot for tugging on shoes and socks.

To prevent morning traffic problems, replace a single sink with two separate vanities. Give yourself additional luxury in less space by adding a steam shower instead of a whirlpool tub. The steam shower in this expanded bath fills what was once closet space and includes two showerheads.

## DESIGNER TIP

If you don't have a porch roof to look toward, consider adding a cantilevered bump-out. Cantilevered bump-outs do not require their own foundation, so they are typically more affordable than additions that require adding on to the home's foundation. (See pages 70–71 and page 9 for examples of a bath addition created from a cantilevered bumpout.)

Above: Window seats conceal radiators. Bath vanity heights are 36-inches, the same as kitchen counter height. Higher countertops make sense, since both bath and kitchen counters are typically used while standing.

## Take a little, gain a lot

Annexing a small amount of space from an adjoining room may have a minimal effect on that room, yet the change may make a major impact on a small bath's functionality. Since bathrooms are often considered little more than necessity, even some spacious homes have maddeningly tiny baths.

By pushing this sink wall out two feet into the adjoining bedroom, enough space was gained for a roomy vanity cabinet. Prior to the remodeling, the toilet and a wall-hung sink with spindly legs occupied one wall. The bedroom was roomy enough so

### RESURFACE AN OLD TUB

If you don't have the budget or the inclination to replace your tub, consider resurfacing it instead. Whether the tub you have is chipped, stained, or the wrong color, refinishing it can make it look like new—at a fraction of the cost. Specialists offer refinishing services and refinishing kits also are available for avid do-it-yourselfers. When done by a professional, the refinishing process takes four to six hours and requires two to four days of curing. If you're hiring a professional, find one who will guarantee the finish for at least five years.

Two methods of resurfacing are currently available: the latest method involves bonding a thin acrylic liner over the existing tub. The traditional method requires that the surface of the tub be prepared and cleaned and then coated with a special epoxy paint. Painting is less expensive and will run in the neighborhood of $500 to $600. Acrylic liners start at $750.

that borrowing an extra two feet did not affect its function.

To make way for a roomy soaking tub (this tub is 66 inches long as compared to a standard tub which is 60 inches long), the designer took 18 inches from the closet of the bedroom on the opposite side. Because that bedroom is reserved for guest use, a small closet would suffice.

Expanding a bath even minimally can allow for a complete renaissance in style.

Instead of a standard vanity, opt for one that has the look of a fine dresser. Here, a dresser-style cabinet made of cherry serves as the vanity, and wall-hung cabinets flanking the mirror provide plenty of convenient storage. To complete the look, the new tub has a matching wood panel. Painting the walls above the wooden chair rail in a complementary color accents the color of the tile below. Attention to all the details makes a bathroom remodeling successful.

# New use
## Convert

**Above: Because of the roof slope, no wall was tall enough to hold a showerhead. The solution was to hang the showerhead from the ceiling. Quarter round windows soften the severe angles of the sloped roofline and boxy dormers.**

To create an entirely new bath by converting some of your home's existing square footage into a full bath with a tub, toilet, and sink, you'll need a space that measures at least 5x7 feet. If a shower stall is substituted for the tub, the minimum room size can be cut to 3x7 feet. A powder room should be at least 3x6 feet or 4½ feet square. (For more information about space requirements, see Chapter 6, "Elements of Good Design," beginning on page 110.)

You may be able to add a new bath to existing square footage, including contractor fees and materials, for $6,000 to $7,000, depending on where you live. The main question—in terms of cost—is where you'll locate the new toilet. If the new fixture cannot be easily plumbed into the existing vent stack, the resulting complications can add thousands of dollars to your remodeling cost. Laundry areas are considered good candidates for conversions because they're already equipped with plumbing. For an attic or basement conversion, it's most economical if you can stack a new bathroom directly over or under an existing one. Attic conversions may require adding or changing roof trusses or beefing up the roof framing.

### DESIGNER TIP

If a low ceiling prevents you from putting the showerhead as high on the wall as you would like it, install an overhead shower fixture like the one shown, *left*, instead. Overhead fixtures also reduce wall splashes, so you may not need a shower door, curtain, or even shower walls.

The bath shown here was created from existing square footage in the attic of a 1927 Dutch Colonial home. Two shed roof dormers, equipped with classic six-over-six windows, suit the style of the house and create the headroom needed to launch a complete third-story retreat. One new dormer shelters a new stairwell and the master bath vanity area; the other envelops a new bedroom sitting area. The narrower space between the dormers serves as a hallway connecting the bedroom and bath.

To enjoy the look of pedestal sinks but not give up the storage a vanity provides, install a storage hutch between the two sinks like the owners of this bath did. If you don't like cleaning shower curtains or doors, create an open shower similar to the one *above left*. The showerhead hangs from the ceiling so that the water sprays downward instead of sideways, minimizing splash.

A window seat adds a whimsical touch to the bath. Open shelves below provide storage for books and towels. A glass-topped coffee table, a planting urn, an old-fashioned lamp, and colorful fabrics and rugs bring living-room warmth to the utilitarian space.

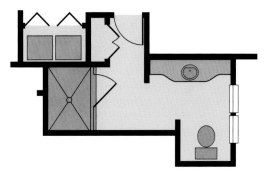

## Trade two for one

Underused spare bedrooms are excellent candidates for gaining the space needed for a new master bath. The bath featured here was created by converting two existing bedrooms into one spacious master suite. The shower, vanity, and toilet tuck into separate, widely spaced existing alcoves, leaving the midsection free for dressing and for in-and-out traffic.

When a standard-depth vanity will infringe too much on floor space, a vanity with a stair-step shape, such as the one *below,* often is the solution. The vanity hugs an inside wall, leaving room on the exterior wall for large double-hung windows. The solid-surface countertop follows the base cabinet's shape, jogging inward a few inches to accommodate the windows at one end and to ease traffic bottlenecks at the other.

To make way for a double-size shower, complete with wall-mounted sprays and lever controls at each end, may require nixing another luxury, such as a whirlpool tub or a second sink.

**Right: Whitewashed maple, soft grays, and an oversize window create an open, airy look in this small bath. A maple-framed alcove adds a custom touch to the bath's vanity area. A gray-and-white checkerboard pattern adds a dash of drama to the tile floor.**

## TO WHIRL OR NOT TO WHIRL?

Soothing sore muscles or frazzled nerves in a bubbling tub is definitely appealing, but will you take the time to use it? If not, you may be better off with a roomy steam shower or smaller soaking tub. Keep in mind that large whirlpool tubs take a long time to fill, are often noisy, and may require added structural support because they are extremely heavy when filled. You may also need a larger (or second) hot water heater to fill the tub while keeping the hot water flowing to other rooms in the house. If a whirlpool is a must-have in your new bath, make sure you insulate the room for sound and/or spend the extra money for a quieter model.

Above: **Stone-look ceramic tile and ogee trim merge the double-size shower stall with the rest of the bath. A wooden loveseat makes dressing in the bath a more comfortable proposition.**

# New Space
## Addition

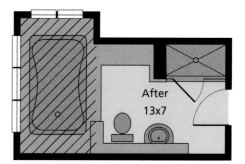

Adding a bath to the exterior of your house is generally more expensive than finding room for one inside, but if you don't have space to spare, an addition may be the only choice. A bump-out, a simple extension that can be cantilevered, is less expensive than an addition that requires its own foundation.

In the bath featured here, the homeowners cantilevered a small bump-out in the place where a small deck once was. The point where the ceiling drops above the tub marks the spot of the old exterior wall. That wall was simply pushed out about 5 feet, annexing approximately 35 square feet.

Plumbing is expensive, so to keep costs down, leave as many fixtures as you can in their existing locations. In this bath, the toilet and pedestal sink did not move, and that freed up some of the budget for luxurious details. To provide additional counter space

**Below: A vanity cabinet would have encroached on this bath's new, more expansive feel. Instead, a slender pedestal sink—recycled from the previous bath—makes a standout statement. The shelf that stretches behind the sink is new. Opposite the sink, convenient hooks keep terrycloth robes and towels close.**

///// added space

for toiletries, add a narrow shelf to the wall above the sink.

Standard-size vanities and such are sized for standard-size bathrooms. Uniquely shaped spaces may require custom-built cabinets or shower enclosures to maximize the room's useable space. The tiled shower in this bath is only 26 inches wide, but its 4-foot length and custom glass enclosure make it feel roomy.

If possible, include a shower seat for safety and convenience. For small showers, at least include a small shelf about 18 inches above the floor. Besides holding shower clutter, the shelf serves as a footrest for shaving legs safely.

### MAXIMIZE COMFORT

**Ventilate.** Proper ventilation keeps your bath free of mildew and moisture damage. Install overhead fans and operable windows to let air in and moisture out. Choose a ventilating fan that exchanges all the air in the room eight times or more per hour.

**Add convenience.** Allow at least 24 inches of towel-bar space for each person. Plan a towel bar no farther than 6 inches from the tub or shower entrance. Find room for a seat that enables you to towel off and dress comfortably.

**Plan door swings.** Reversing the swing of this bath's entry door eliminated conflict with the new shower door. Consider the direction of cabinet door swings, too.

**Right:** To prevent the 9x10-foot bath from looking crowded, both the shower and tub areas are open. To keep the decor light and airy the designer chose shades of off-white and linen combined with soft green tile accents.

**Below right:** A pocket door replaces the old closet door, saving space and preventing collisions with the hall door.

After
9x10

added space

## Keep it simple

To gain more square footage than a bump-out can provide, look for ways to add on without disrupting the traffic flow in other rooms. This bath was added on to the back of a 1925 rambler, connecting to the master bedroom through what had been a closet.

Make the new space match the old as closely as possible. Here, new bath windows are the same as others along the rear of the house. Even a new glass block window in the shower stall—which is the only glass block in the house—appears consistent because it's tall and skinny.

Take design cues from those already established throughout the existing house. The home in which this bath resides has a distinctly Spanish flavor. The owner chose to bring that theme out in the new bath by utilizing earthy colors and natural materials. Limestone covers the vanity counters. The floor is mottled glazed tile, a material repeated in all three of the home's bathrooms. Decorative wall tiles also play up the Spanish theme. Tongue-and-groove pine paneling covers the ceiling.

Trade off openness and privacy as necessary to keep your new bath feeling comfortable, but not crowded. In this bath, the toilet is in a niche at the end of the vanity as opposed to having its own private closet. Conserve floor space by replacing swinging doors with pocket ones. And use wall-hung cabinets and freestanding furniture pieces to increase storage.

Left: A combination of handheld and built-in showerheads adds comfort and offers flexibility. For architectural interest, tiles above the chair rail are larger than those below it. To cut costs, decorative tiles are used sparingly in the shower.

# Surfaces
## Cabinetry
## Fixtures

Choose materials and fixtures wisely so that your new bath will look great and perform beautifully.

**Opposite: Freestanding furniture pieces add sitting room charm to an often austere-looking room. Here, an old-fashioned beaded-board tub surround, two-tone tile floors, flowing fabrics; soft blues; and a smattering of antiques set the style. Combined with a collage of botanical prints, these elements conspire to give this bath a seaside cottage feel.**

Material choices, such as flooring, countertops, and wall coverings, affect the look, the function, and the cost of your bathroom remodeling. The essential components include sinks, tubs, showers, and toilets. As such, they need to be durable as well as practical and attractive.

Your top priority when choosing these bath components should be how the materials will function given how you, your family, and guests will use the bathroom. Your best dollar payback will come from equipping your bath with materials, fixtures, and features that have become the standard in comparably priced homes. If you're planning to live in the house for years and resale is less of an issue, make material choices that are as personal as you please.

# Flooring

Kitchen and bath floors are probably the hardest working surfaces in your home. They must withstand plenty of abuse: overflowing sinks and bathtubs; wet feet, heavy foot traffic, and garden dirt, to name a few. To determine what flooring will work best for you, consider three major criteria: what you need in terms of wear and tear, how the floor will fit into your design, and whether your selection will fit into your budget.

## Laminate

While laminate has been used for countertops for decades, it has only been available as a flooring material for a few years. Slightly less expensive than its authentic counterparts, laminate flooring is known for its durability and ease of cleanup, but it does have a slight hollow feel underfoot. It can be installed over existing flooring. Not all laminates are suitable for installation in moisture-prone rooms, so be sure to check the manufacturer's warranty before purchasing. Unfortunately, it can not be refinished if damaged.

Laminate flooring is made from a complex layering process that includes a clear, extremely durable, aluminum oxide top coat; a second layer of plastic resin embedded into a decorative photographic image; a rigid back core, such as medium- or high-density fiberboard;

*Below:* **Vinyl sheeting and tiles are durable, easy on your feet, and easy to clean. They are a great choice for kids' baths, but all but the most expensive vinyl flooring can be dented or cut if a heavy or sharp object falls on it.**

### THE FLOOR BENEATH THE FLOOR

Before installing any new floor, you must check the condition of the subfloor (the material between the floor covering and the floor joists) and the supporting joists. Decayed subflooring, especially around the toilet and tub, is a common problem in older homes. Spot repairs may be adequate, but in some cases, you may need to replace the entire subfloor.

Unless you can inspect the underside of the subfloor from the basement, you'll have to pry up a bit of the existing floor covering to inspect the subfloor below it. Prod around the base of fixtures and cabinets with a screwdriver in search of soft spots. Check with a professional if you are unsure of how you should proceed.

and a backing material designed to prevent warping. Because the decorative image printed on the second layer is a photograph, laminate floors truly look like the wood, stone, or ceramic tile they were designed to impersonate. Laminate comes in three shapes—planks, squares, and rectangles. Oak is the hottest seller, followed by maple. Ceramic tile and natural stone look-alikes are also available. Prices range from $18 to $45 per square yard; add $27 to $36 per square yard for professional installation.

## Ceramic tile

Clay-base ceramic tiles provide the ideal choice for moisture-prone areas. Floor tiles are extremely durable; water, stain, and wear resistant; and easy to care for. They come in an array of colors, patterns, shapes, and sizes. Tiles 12 inches square or larger are currently the most popular choice. Although tile can feel cold underfoot, it can be warmed with radiant heat coils. For safety purposes, always choose a bath tile that has a slip-resistant finish. Seal all tile grout; otherwise, it can be difficult to clean. Broken tiles cannot be repaired, but they can be replaced.

Ceramic tile costs range from less than $9 per square yard for mass-produced tiles to hundreds of dollars per square yard for commissioned art tiles. To prevent chipping and cracking, install tile only over a firmly supported subflooring. Uncomplicated installations costs start at about $9 per square yard and top out at $45 or more per yard for more complicated installations.

## Stone tile

Stone tiles are similar to those used in building construction centuries ago. These tiles are made by slicing boulders and slabs of natural rock into thin squares or rectangles. Not all stone is suitable for use as bath flooring, however. Glossy surfaces require regular polishing and can be slippery when wet. Marble tiles must be sealed to prevent staining and pitting. (Splashed urine will damage

marble.) Limestone and slate tiles are also porous; they too must be sealed to prevent dirt and stain absorption. Granite tiles require little or no maintenance; they are nonporous, easy to clean, and virtually indestructible. For better traction, choose a honed finish.

Like its ceramic counterpart, stone tile needs an extremely stable subsurface that does not give. Stone tile prices vary by region, depending on how far the stone must

**Left:** Tumbled marble tiles in various natural shades inset in limestone give the flooring a highly decorative appearance. The complexity of this stone pattern adds a significant amount to the installation costs. Because the finish is dull, dirt and grime are difficult to see. **Below:** Colorful diamond-shape ceramic insets enliven this bath's mostly white tile walls.

be shipped. Installation prices range from $9 to $45 per square yard.

### Concrete

Able to withstand the rigors of heavy traffic, concrete is becoming a popular surface for much-used areas of the home. Easy to clean and versatile, concrete also can mimic the look of stone, at a lower cost.

Concrete can be dyed virtually any color, and before it is fully cured it can be stamped to create any sort of surface texture or appearance. Because concrete is very porous, it must be sealed for protection against embedded dirt and stains. Concrete flooring ranges from $36 to $90 per square yard, installed. (Stamping and etching drive up the cost.)

### Hardwood

The most familiar type of hardwood flooring is composed of solid, one-piece boards. But there is also a variety called *engineered* wood flooring that consists of two or more layers of

## Flooring Options at a Glance

| MATERIAL | ADVANTAGES | DISADVANTAGES | COSTS |
|---|---|---|---|
| LAMINATE | Durable; can be installed over existing floor; easy to clean and maintain; wide range of colors and designs imitate wood, stone, or ceramic tile | Although extremely durable, it cannot be refinished if damaged; floor can be noisy unless foam underlayment is used | $18–$45 per square yard; add $27–$36 per square yard for professional installation |
| CERAMIC TILE | Durable; water and stain resistant; wide choice of colors, designs, textures, and shapes (tiles can be mixed for border treatments and field accents) | Can be cold and noisy: glazed tiles can be slippery when wet; hard on feet; moisture and dirt can get into grout joints and tiles can stain unless they're sealed; difficult, but possible to repair | $9 per square yard on up. For professional installation, add anywhere from $9–$45 per square yard, depending on complexity of installation |
| STONE TILE | Virtually indestructible; easy to maintain; elegant; withstands high temperatures | Marble is cold and slippery; hard on feet; expensive; strong subfloor needed; must be sealed; limestone and granite readily absorb stains and dirt; difficult to repair; gloss surfaces require regular polishing, which is costly and messy | Vary by region, depending upon how far the stone must be shipped; prices to install prices range from $9–$45 per square yard |
| CONCRETE | Hard wearing, long lasting; easy to clean; versatile and colorful | Prone to staining and cracking although hairline cracks do not affect the material's actual strength; can feel cold and hard on feet; requires regular sealing treatments | $36–$90 per square foot, installed; stamping and etching drive up the cost |
| HARDWOOD | Wear resistant; lasts indefinitely; provides a natural, warm look; comfortable; surface finish easy to keep clean; can be refinished | Vulnerable to moisture; some woods such as pine dent easily; may darken with age; waxed surfaces can't be mopped; some finishes wear unevenly and are difficult to repair | $27–$45 per square yard; installation prices range from $18 to $45 per square yard |
| RESILIENT | Comfortable; water and stain resistant; easy to install (tiles easier than sheets); simple to clean (polyurethane finishes preclude waxing); large number of designs (tiles can be mixed to create custom patterns or color accents); sheets up to 12 feet wide eliminate seams in smaller rooms | Soft (prone to dent and tear); warranty no longer than 10 years; moisture can get into seams between tiles; doesn't wear as well as other flooring (inlaid pattern in vinyl lasts longer than pattern applied photographically) | $9–$38 per square yard; add a $1 per square yard for installation. Linoleum runs $40-$43 per square yard; add $2 per square yard for installation |
| CARPET | Slip resistant; warm and comfortable; muffles sound; wide range of colors and styles; used primarily in dry climates, such as in the Southwest | Absorbs water; stains easily; promotes mildew growth; not easy to clean (use short-pile and unsculptured types; nylon and other synthetics are washable) | $3 per square yard for polyester to $90 per square yard for the finest wool; cushion prices vary from $2.50 to $6 per square yard; installation costs start at $2 per square yard |

look. Because the floor is not as hard as ceramic or stone, it is more comfortable to walk on.

All hardwood, whether it is solid or engineered, is vulnerable to moisture. Today's polyurethane finishes stand up to limited amounts of water. You'll want to avoid using hardwood in children's baths or in any bath where excess water is unavoidable. Engineered wood and solid wood floor prices are similar; the cost per square yard ranges from $27 to $45 per square yard. Installation prices range from $18 to $45 per square yard.

## Resilient

All synthetic, resin-based floor coverings come under the resilient flooring category. Resilient flooring includes vinyl tiles and sheet flooring. Sheets up to 15 feet wide eliminate seams in most bathrooms. Once-popular, linoleum has been long out of favor but is making a comeback as it is considered an eco-friendly choice.

Resilient flooring is an excellent choice if you have young children. It's flexible, water

wood laminated together—similar to plywood. The top layers consist of a hardwood veneer; the bottom layers are typically made from softer woods. Due to the limited thickness of the top layer, these engineered woods can be refinished a limited number of times, but they are generally considered more stable for moisture-filled bath installations. Both engineered and solid woods are wear resistant, and they provide a naturally warm

**Left: Hardwood flooring adds a warm look to a cool bath, but unlike most other flooring types, wood cannot be physically warmed via radiant-heat as discussed** *below*.

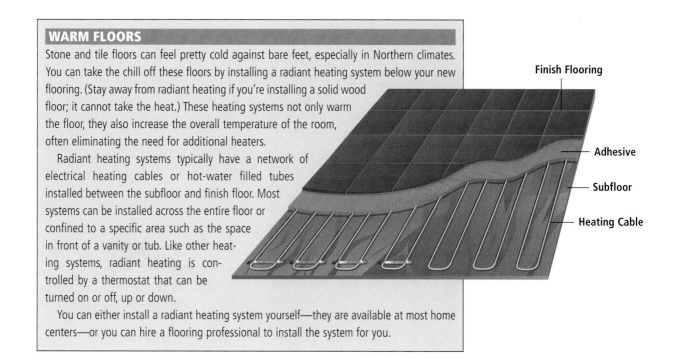

**WARM FLOORS**

Stone and tile floors can feel pretty cold against bare feet, especially in Northern climates. You can take the chill off these floors by installing a radiant heating system below your new flooring. (Stay away from radiant heating if you're installing a solid wood floor; it cannot take the heat.) These heating systems not only warm the floor, they also increase the overall temperature of the room, often eliminating the need for additional heaters.

Radiant heating systems typically have a network of electrical heating cables or hot-water filled tubes installed between the subfloor and finish floor. Most systems can be installed across the entire floor or confined to a specific area such as the space in front of a vanity or tub. Like other heating systems, radiant heating is controlled by a thermostat that can be turned on or off, up or down.

You can either install a radiant heating system yourself—they are available at most home centers—or you can hire a flooring professional to install the system for you.

Finish Flooring

Adhesive

Subfloor

Heating Cable

Below: Like laminate countertops, laminate floors look very much like that natural wood or stone they imitate. Oak laminate is the most popular and it can be installed over existing flooring. Choose a laminate that is designed for use in moisture-prone areas.

and stain resistant, and easy to maintain. Because the flooring is relatively soft, it helps muffle noise and is easy on the feet and legs. The softness of the flooring, however, almost makes it prone to denting. Most warranties last no longer than 10 years. Inlaid patterns wear better than patterns applied photographically, as the inlaid image runs through-

out the thickness of the material. Vinyl prices range from $9 to $38 per square yard; add a dollar per square yard for installation. Linoleum runs from $40 to $43 per square yard; add $2 per square yard for installation.

## Carpet

Slip resistant, warm, and comfortable, carpet muffles sounds. Because it absorbs water, stains easily, and promotes mildew growth,

it is usually not recommended for bath installations, particularly in areas adjacent to the toilet, tub, or shower. If you like the feel of carpet underfoot, use washable rugs or have a washable or dry-cleanable carpet runner custom-made, like the one shown *left*, to cover the vanity's floor area.

Carpet is typically made from one of four fibers: nylon, olefin, polyester, or wool. Wool is typically the most expensive and most durable (although is it not washable), followed by nylon, polypropylene (also referred to as olefin), and polyester respectively. Nylon and other synthetics are washable. Loop piles will perform better than cut piles over the long haul because the loops help evenly distribute the impact of foot traffic.

Carpet prices range from a few dollars a square yard for polyester to upwards of $90 per square yard for the finest wool. Decent quality nylon carpets range in price from $15 to $30 per square yard. Cushion prices vary from $2.50 to $6 per square yard. Installation costs start at $2 per square yard and go upward depending on the job's complexity.

**Left: Although commonly installed in bathrooms during the 1980s and early 1990s, wall-to-wall carpeting is no longer recommended for use in the bath because it traps the moisture that causes mildew. Removable runners that can be machine washed or dry-cleaned are better choices.**

## DECISION MAKERS

- **Allergies:** If you're particularly sensitive and concerned about your home's indoor air quality, choose a hard flooring material, such as ceramic tile or hardwood that contains few crevices or grooves to harbor dust mites and allergens. Avoid installing carpeting, as it can harbor mildew and germs. Look for finishes that have been treated with an antimicrobial chemical designed to reduce the growth of bacteria, viruses, and other microbes.
- **Cleanability:** For easy-care flooring, choose vinyl, laminate, ceramic or stone tile—smooth surfaces that clean up with a sweep and a rag. Other materials will require a bit more upkeep to maintain their good looks.
- **Durability:** With the ability to endure an onslaught of abuse from water, children, pets, and heavy traffic, flooring materials made of ceramic and stone tile, laminate, and concrete rank at the top. Although marks will show on hardwood, the surface can be refinished.
- **Longevity:** Standing the test of time are stone and ceramic tiles, hardwood, and concrete. Most other flooring materials will eventually need replacing.

Available in multiple patterns and colors, textures range from smooth and glossy to a mottled, leatherlike look. Stone-look finishes are currently the most popular.

Fabricated laminated countertops come in two forms: prefab or special order. These fabricated counters are made from bonding laminate sheeting over a ¾-inch-thick particleboard core. Exposed edges can be adorned with matching laminate or with a contrasting decorative edging. Installing the finished countertop is not difficult, although larger pieces can be somewhat bulky and difficult to handle. It is also possible to buy sheets of laminate material and then attach it to a particleboard counter yourself, but this takes special tools and can be somewhat time consuming. A professional will likely do the best job. Prices for laminate countertops range from $27 to $60 per running foot, installed.

## Ceramic tile

As they do for walls and floors, clay-base ceramic tiles make an attractive, durable finish for countertops, especially in moisture-prone areas. The surface tiles are durable; water, stain, and wear resistant; and easy to care for. Heat from rollers or curling irons won't cause damage. They are available in an

**Above: Laminate often resembles the look of a natural material such as stone or wood as shown. It is also available in bright colors that will enliven any bath.**

**Right: Ceramic tile is extremely durable and it is available in more colors than laminate. To prevent grout from appearing stained or dirty, choose a dark color grout and have it properly sealed.**

Countertops are available in a large number of styles and materials—each with its own set of properties. Look for something that will stand up to water, soap, alcohol- and acetone-based liquids, toothpaste, and cosmetics.

## Laminate

Affordably priced, laminate is still the most widely used countertop surfacing material. Similar in construction to laminate floors, these countertops are made from layers of plastic sheeting and particle board bonded together under heat and pressure. Laminate countertops clean easily and are resistant to water and stains. They do scratch, can wear thin, and dull over time. Hard blows can chip or dent the plastic; a damaged counter cannot be repaired.

Left: Slate tiles add texture to this bath counter. The natural stone is extremely durable and less porous than marble. The stone is available in varying shades of gray and black.

array of colors, patterns, shapes, and sizes. As with tile flooring, tile grout, if left unsealed, can encourage mildew growth and be difficult to clean.

Ceramic tile costs range from $18 to $90 per linear foot, installed.

## Solid surfacing

Cast from an acrylic resin, solid-surface countertops require little maintenance and are more durable than laminate. Intense heat and heavy, falling objects (an unlikely occurrence in the bathroom) can cause damage, but scratches, abrasions, and minor burns can be repaired with fine-grade sandpaper. Solid surface countertops are available in more colors and styles than ever before; the most popular finish is white followed by stone imitations. Edge treatments range from a simple smooth edge that imitates stone to intricate inlaid designs in contrasting colors. Sinks can be integrated directly

# Countertop Options at a Glance

| MATERIAL | ADVANTAGES | DISADVANTAGES | COSTS |
| --- | --- | --- | --- |
| LAMINATE | Durable; inexpensive; easy to clean and maintain; wide range of colors and designs imitate wood, stone, or ceramic tile | Although durable, it does scratch and it cannot be refinished if damaged | $26–60 per running foot, installed |
| CERAMIC TILE | Durable; water and stain resistant; wide choice of colors, designs, textures, and shapes (tiles can be mixed for border treatments and field accents) | Moisture and dirt can get into grout joints, and tiles can stain unless they're sealed; very hard; if you drop glass items on the counter they will most likely break; difficult, but possible to repair | $18–$90 per linear foot, installed |
| STONE SLAB | Virtually indestructible; easy to maintain, especially granite; elegant; withstands high temperatures | Expensive; marble and limestone readily absorb stains and dirt; difficult to repair; gloss surfaces require regular polishing, which is costly and messy | Vary by region, depending on how far the stone must be shipped; for most areas of the country estimate $125–$250 per running foot, installed |
| CONCRETE | Hard wearing, long lasting; easy to clean; versatile and colorful | Prone to staining and cracking although hairline cracks do not affect the materials actual strength; requires regular sealing treatments | $70-$150 per linear foot, installed; stamping and etching drive up the cost |
| HARDWOOD | Wear resistant; lasts indefinitely; provides a natural, warm look; surface finish easy to keep clean; can be refinished | Vulnerable to moisture; some woods such as pine dent easily; may darken with age; some finishes wear unevenly and are difficult to repair | $40–$75 per linear foot, installed |

Below: **A limestone slab adds texture to this bathroom vanity. Because limestone is both light in color and porous, staining can be a problem. Sealing the stone countertop reduces the problem significantly, but it doesn't completely solve it.**

into the countertop—no seams to clean. Prices range from $100 to $250 per linear foot, installed.

### Stone tiles and slabs

Stone countertops are extremely durable; granite resists stains and stands up well to water. It comes in both slab and tile form. Slabs are more expensive, but eliminate grout cleanup. Marble veining, although attractive, makes the marble weaker. Because both marble and limestone like the countertop, *lower left*, are porous stones, they will stain; proper sealing helps but doesn't completely eliminate the problem. Granite is less porous and less likely to stain. Stone counters are available in both slab and tile form; again, tiles are less costly but require grouting and, hence, grout care. Stone slabs run from $125 to $250 per running foot. Tile prices vary greatly.

Cultured marble resembles solid surfacing but is somewhat less expensive. It is made from natural marble embedded in plastic and requires the same care as plastic laminate countertops. Cultured marble is available in sheet form in standard counter dimensions of 19 and 21 inches deep. As with solid surfacing, sinks can be integrated into the countertop. Once scratched, however, cultured marble cannot be repaired. Prices range from $50 to $80 per running foot, installed.

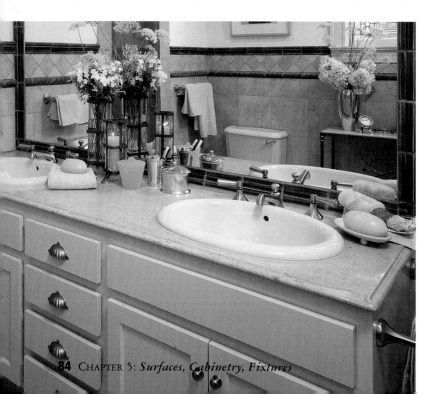

## Concrete

Concrete, although it always has a rough-hewn quality, can be colored, scored, and textured to create many interesting looks. In addition, decorative tiles and metals can be inlaid for a custom look. Sinks can be integrated into the countertop. Because concrete is very porous, however, it must be sealed for protection against embedded dirt and stains. Concrete countertops range from $70 to $150 per linear foot, installed. (Stamping and etching drive up the cost.)

## Wood

Wood counters are attractive, versatile, and easy to install, but they are especially vulnerable to water damage. Their porosity makes them difficult to keep sanitary. Whatever type of wood you choose, you must seal it with marine-quality polyurethane varnish to make it a viable selection for the bath. Special care should be taken to seal around the edges of plumbing fixtures so standing water can't seep in and cause warping or wood rot. Costs for wood countertops range from $40 to $75 per linear foot, installed.

# Surfaces
# Wallcoverings

Surfaces
Wallcoverings

**Below: New painting techniques can make painted walls look just as decorative as wallpaper can. Stenciled-on designs and a combination of latex paint and glaze create the aged look of parchment paper in this painted bath.**

Walls are the largest surface in the bath, so how you adorn them makes a significant impact on the feel of the room. Whether you choose paint, wallpaper, paneling, or tile, remember that your covering of choice for the bathroom must stand up to heat, humidity, and frequent cleaning. Mix and match materials to meet your durability requirements and to create a look that is both attractive and practical.

## Paint

Paint is the least-expensive option and the easiest wallcovering to change whether you tire of it or it starts to look tired. Painting is also an easy do-it-yourself project; the majority of the time involved is spent masking and draping the surfaces you wish to keep paint-free. Combine paint with a latex glaze to create paint treatments that have the look of wallpaper. In the bath *below,* the owners ragged on two tones of paint and

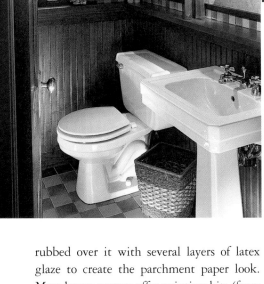

Left: Read the manufacturer's usage recommendations before applying any wallcovering to a bath. Vinyl wallcoverings offer a good choice for bath walls because they are not easily damaged by moisture and they can be wiped clean with a damp cloth. Below: Wood paneling (discussed on page 88) adds natural warmth to a bath. However, if you live in a very humid area and your bath is often filled with steam, you may want to choose a more moisture-resistant wall finish.

terparts. Unlike their alkyd counterparts, latex paints also dry quicker and clean up with soap and water. Look for a paint finish that is washable, scrubbable, and moisture resistant. Paints specified for bathroom use are more expensive but can be worth the investment in terms of durability.

If you want to cover a porcelain, plastic, or tile surface, look for an epoxy paint designated for that specific purpose. Most surfaces must be primed to ensure proper paint adhesion. Quality paint prices range from $20 to $30 per gallon.

## Vinyl wallcoverings

Vinyl wallcoverings (a more durable choice for the bath than wallpapers) come in a vast array of colors, patterns, styles, and textures. Many come with a prepasted adhesive coating that only needs to be dampened to adhere to the wall.

rubbed over it with several layers of latex glaze to create the parchment paper look. Most home centers offer painting kits (from $30 to $70 each) that include the instructions and the necessary tools to create a number of painting techniques, such as sponging or rag rolling.

Today's latex water-base paints are as durable as many of their alkyd oil-base coun-

When it comes to the bath, it's best to choose a vinyl covering that is laminated to a fabric backing instead of a covering that is all or partly paper. Vinyl coverings withstand moisture much better than papers do. Products labeled "scrubbable" are the most durable and will tolerate more abrasion than the "washable" ones. Although not recommended, standard wallpapers can be used in half baths or in areas of the bath that are not subjected to splashes or condensation. Wallcovering prices range from $20 to $150 or more per single roll. Coverings from major manufacturers typically run from $25 to $40 per roll.

### Wood paneling

Wood adds a natural warmth that complements many interior design themes. As a wall-surfacing material, it comes in the form of pre-milled solid wainscoting or tongue-and-groove beaded board, veneered plywood, or melamine-surfaced hardboard. Both solid wood and plywood-backed veneers must be sealed with a water-resistant coating, such as polyurethane. Hardboard panels coated with melamine (a thin layer of white plastic) are well suited for baths because melamine is water resistant and easy to clean.

### Tile

Ceramic and natural stone tiles are attractive, durable, and easy to clean. Most are stain resistant and, when installed correctly, full-waterproof. Although ceramic wallcoverings are more expensive than those previously discussed, their longevity may make

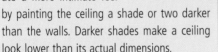
them worth considering for at least the wettest areas of the bath.

Like floor and countertop tiles, wall tiles come glazed and unglazed, plain and patterned, and in a vast array of colors. Stock tiles can be mixed and matched with custom-painted tiles to create an individual look. Wall tiles are not as durable as floor and countertop tiles because they typically do not have to withstand the same kind of abuse. Because of this, you may use floor and countertop tiles on the walls, but you should not use wall tiles on the countertops or floors.

You can apply ceramic tile to any dry-wall, plaster, or plywood surface that's smooth, sound, and firm. Unglazed tile may need to be sealed. Slightly less expensive than floor and countertop tile, wall tile prices start at $15 per linear foot, installed, and go up from there.

### Glass block

Glass block is popular because of its sleek spa look and its ability to transmit light while preserving some amount of privacy. It can be used to create walls, shower surrounds, and windows. Glass block costs range from $45 to $65 per square foot, installed.

Below: **These glass block walls are somewhat transparent. You can also find blocks that are nearly opaque, as well as many between these two extremes. Choose the kind of glass block for your bath that best meets your privacy needs.**

# Fixtures
## Sinks

Sinks

Bathroom sinks come in more sizes, shapes, and material choices than ever before. You can purchase round, oval, rectangular, or asymmetrical bowls. Each shape is available in several color choices, although white still outsells all the other colors combined. Some of the more expensive models are adorned with hand-painted designs. Or indulge in having a standard sink custom-painted to match your decor.

Before you choose the right one (or two) for your bath, consider how often the sink will be used. Sinks used in half baths and full guest baths typically receive less use, so durability and maintenance are lesser issues in these spaces than in master baths and children's baths.

In frequently used baths, choose materials to match the kind of wear and tear your family will instigate. Choose larger, deeper

**Below:** Vessel sinks sit on top of the counter like a bowl. Most require wall-mounted faucets and a specialized drainpipe fitting.

**Right:** It's all in the details: Since everything is exposed on this sink, the pipes and underside of the bowl are cleanly finished.

Left: A wall-hung sink is a good choice for a snug space. This sink's old-fashioned good looks make it suitable for either traditional or country-style baths.

sinks to reduce splashing and countertop cleanup. To ensure a good match in terms of design, consider purchasing a matching sink, toilet, and bathtub.

## Materials

The most common materials choices are:

- **Porcelain-enameled cast iron.** These sinks are extremely durable and easy to care for, but are somewhat heavy and require a sturdy support system.
- **Vitreous china.** Having a lustrous surface, these sinks are not as heavy as porcelain-enameled cast-iron sinks, and are the most resistant to discoloration and corrosion. They, however, can be chipped or cracked when struck by a heavy object.
- **Solid surface.** These sinks offer varying degrees of durability based on the material from which they are made. Sinks made from the same acrylic resin as quality solid-surface countertops are the most durable and require little maintenance. Polyester and cultured marble sinks share similar properties but scratch and dull more readily. Any of these

sinks may be integrated directly into the countertop. A fine-grade sandpaper will remove shallow nicks and scratches.

■ **Stainless steel.** Durable and unaffected by household chemicals, stainless-steel sinks like the one shown *opposite* do tend to show hardwater and soap spots.

■ **Glass.** Glass sinks like the undermount version shown *opposite* are becoming popular. Although they do require extra care to prevent scratching or breaking, their smooth finish is easy to clean. Frosted glass shows water spotting less than its clear counterpart.

## Styles

Styles of sinks fall into three main categories:

■ **Pedestal.** These sinks fit on top of a pedestal-shaped base and are an ideal solution for a small bath. The disadvantage of a pedestal sink is that it offers little counterspace and no base cabinet storage below. Simple pedestals start at $125.

■ **Wall hung.** Like pedestal sinks, wall-hung styles, such as the ones shown on page 91, have the advantage of squeezing into small spaces. They have the same disadvantages of pedestal sinks with one more—there is no pedestal to hide any plumbing lines. To make up for this, some sinks have brass legs to offer a more finished look underneath. Wall-hung sinks are often the preferred choice in universally designed baths because they can be installed at any height and have a clear space underneath that allows for seated knee space and wheelchair access. These sinks start at $80.

■ **Vanity sinks.** Vanity sinks have lots of countertop space around them as well as cabinet storage below. Vanity sinks, however, require the most floor space of any sink style. Vanity sinks can be installed in several ways:

—*Vessel sinks*, as shown on page 90, are the latest design introduction. These sinks appear to sit atop the vanity counter, much like a bowl on a table; in reality, most often they rest in a custom-cut hole in the vanity top. Prices range from $300 to $700 for most models.

*Below: A self-rimming sink is easy to install because the hole does not have to be perfectly cut.*

Left: Undermounted below the stone countertop, this sink requires a perfect cut in the stone. The smooth counter makes it easy to wipe spills directly into the sink, although the seam may require a little extra care when cleaning. Below: This glass undermount sink is lit from below for a dazzling nightlight.

—*Integral sinks* are part of the same material as the vanity counter. Because there is no joint between the bowl and the countertop, they are easy to clean. If either the sink or counter is damaged beyond repair, the entire unit must be replaced. Prices range from $200 to $500.

—*Self-rimming* or surface-mounted sinks as shown *opposite* have a top edge that rests on top of the counter after the sink is dropped into a hole large enough to accommodate the sink bowl. The rim forms a tight seal with the countertop to prevent leaks. These sinks are the easiest to install because the hole need not be a perfect cut as it is hidden below the rim once the sink is in place. Prices for basic drop-in sinks start at $75.

—*Undermounted sinks,* as shown *above,* are attached to the bottom of the countertop, creating a clean, tailored look. Like rimmed sinks, they can be somewhat difficult to clean underneath the lip where the sink and counter seals together. They require an exact cut for installation. Similar in price to drop-ins, these sinks start at $75.

—*Rimmed sinks* sit slightly above the countertop with a tight-fitting metal rim joining the sink and the countertop. The rim is made of different finishes to match whatever type of faucet you select. Rimmed sinks can be difficult to clean around the seal and require a nearly perfect cut for installation. These sinks are the least expensive; prices start at $70.

# Fixtures
## Faucets

As you shop for faucets, you'll see everything from traditional, two-handled models that look much like they did a century ago to the newest one-handle creations that look like modern sculpture. Don't make a selection based on looks alone; durability is the key to your continued satisfaction. You'll also need to make sure that the faucet set you select is the proper size and design to fit your sink. Most vanity sinks come with holes drilled in their rims to accommodate standard faucets and plumbing. These three basic faucet styles are designed to fit the predrilled holes:

■ **Single-handle faucets.** These faucets have one spout and one handle, as the one shown *opposite,* that controls the flow of both hot and cold water.

■ **Center-set faucets.** With a spout and handle(s) in one unit, these faucets may have either single-handle or double-handle controls. Most are designed for a three-hole basin, with the outside holes spaced 4 inches from center to center. However, some have a single-post design that requires only one hole.

■ **Spread-fit faucets.** These faucets separate spout and handles, as shown *left.* The connection between them is concealed below the sink deck. They can be adapted to fit holes spaced from 4 to 10 inches apart. They can be individualized even more if they are mounted on a countertop next to the sink.

*Above:* **Spread-fit faucets provide some design flexibility in that you can choose (within 10 inches) just how much space you want between the handles and the spout.**

## Faucet and Showerhead Finish Options

| FINISH | ADVANTAGES | DISADVANTAGES |
|---|---|---|
| **Chrome** (polished, brushed, or matte) | Polished chrome is extremely hard, easily cleaned and doesn't oxidize; matte chrome has a softer appearance and is as durable as polished chrome | Inexpensive chrome sprayed over plastic parts tends to peel |
| **Brass** (polished, satin finish, or antique finish) | Classy look; titanium finishes resist scratching, fading, and corrosion | Standard brass finishes are prone to scratching, tarnishing, and corrosion |
| **Baked on enamel or epoxy coatings** (available in many colors) | Wide choice of colors; easy to clean | May chip or fade; some chemicals may damage color |
| **Gold plate** (polished, brushed, or matte) | Great visual appeal; quality gold won't tarnish; matte finishes hide scratches | Expensive; quality varies; finish must be sealed by manufacturer or the gold can be damaged |
| **Other metals** (polished, brushed, or matte) | Metals like nickel also offer great visual appeal and durability | Like gold plate, these metals can be expensive; quality varies by the manufacturer |

For example, the spout can be placed on a rear corner and the handles off to one side. These faucets are handy for tight installations where there is not enough room for a full faucet at the back of the sink basin. They are also ideal for whirlpool tubs, so that the handles are accessible from outside the tub for filling.

■ **Wall-mount faucets.** A fourth faucet type is attached to the wall as opposed to the sink or the counter, as shown above the stainless-steel sink on page 93. These faucets were designed for unusually shaped sinks, such as old-fashioned farm sinks, antique bowls, or other vessels that have been modified for use in the bath.

### What's inside counts

Faucet prices start at $50 for the most basic models and can run as high as $500 to $600 or more for a waterfall tub faucet. Solid-brass, die-cast innards are a sign of quality, but often come with a hefty price tag—anywhere from $250 to $500 or more. Beware of faucets with plastic shells or handles.

### ONE HANDLE OR TWO?

Both popular design choices, one-handle designs are easier to use than their two-handle counterparts. With a little practice on a one-handle model, you can find the temperature you want on the first try. You can also turn the water on with your elbow or wrist when your hands are full or dirty.

Two-handle faucets, on the other hand, offer a more traditional look and you can combine different handles and spouts for a custom look.

Although appealing in price, their durability may be disappointing.

Faucet mechanisms have come a long way beyond the simple valve stem with replaceable washers that wore out every few years (although this type of faucet is still on the market today). Precision metal parts, synthetic materials, and hard ceramics have made the washerless faucet commonplace, and on those rare occasions when maintenance is required, the repair is a simple matter of replacing a modular assembly. Ceramic disk faucets can go from off to a full torrent in only a quarter turn of the handle.

# Showerheads

This handheld showerhead can be clipped in place for a traditional shower or unhooked to use in a fashion similar to a garden hose, spraying the water directly where you want it.

More showers are being equipped with a combination of shower-heads as opposed to a single wall-mount unit. All showerheads are rated according to to flow rate, or the number of gallons of water they spray per minute (gpm). Water-consuming showerheads deliver as many as 8 gpms. Low-flow models use just 2.5 gpms and today's low-flow models do just as good a job of cleaning as their water-consuming counterparts. Your home's water pressure is also a factor. Either shower-head type can be adjusted for a spray that varies from fine to coarse, and a water action that ranges from a gentle pulsation to a vigorous massage.

The following types of spray heads are available:

■ **Standard wall-mount showerhead.** These heads are the most economical and can be adjusted slightly by moving the shower neck. Models that offer varying spray types fit the needs of most users.

■ **Top-mount showerhead.** These shower-heads work well in areas where the ceiling is too low to accommodate a wall-mount head (see page 66 for an example). Because the

## PLUMBING LAYOUTS

When placing fixtures in your bathroom, think about how they are used and in what order. The sink, for example, should be positioned closest to the door because it's often the only fixture used or the last stop in most people's bathing routines. The tub and shower can be farthest from the door because they are not used as frequently.

How you lay out your fixtures can also affect your plumbing bill. The fewer "wet walls" you have, the less costly your plumbing bill will be. One-wall layouts, with fixtures arranged along a single wall, are the simplest and require the fewest plumbing fittings. If you are unhappy with the functionality of a one wet-wall bath, the money you save may cost you another remodeling in the future.

• **One-Wall Layout.** A design with all the supply and draining pipes located within one wall is more cost efficient but limits your design possibilities. You may want to consider this layout if you are creating an entirely new bath space and have to supply water to the area.

• **Two-Wall Layout.** A design with plumbing in two walls requires more plumbing work but offers more floor area and storage space around the sink.

• **Three-Wall Layout.** Three-wall layouts offer the most design flexibility, but they require more space and more complex plumbing systems.

users to quickly wash without getting their hair wet.

■ **Body spa shower panels.** These panels are installed against one or more walls of the shower stall and are equipped with water jets arranged vertically from knee to neck level. Similar to jets in a whirlpool tub, the water jets pump out and recirculate large quantities of water for a powerful massage.

Most showerhead/faucet handle combinations cost from $75 for a standard model to $1,500 plus for a panel that includes multiple sprays and a handheld showerhead.

Left: A sliding bar showerhead is a good choice in a shared bath where children and adults use the same shower. The head can be easily adjusted to spray higher or lower. Below: This faucet offers a stationary spout and a handheld spray head.

spray comes from overhead, it is difficult to avoid getting your hair wet when washing in this type of shower.

■ **Hand-held showerhead.** These clip-held showerheads are attached to a 3- to 6-foot-long gooseneck hose that enables you to move the spray of water where you want it. The gooseneck hose adds versatility when it comes to washing your hair or rinsing off. And when it comes time to scrub down the shower enclosure, handheld sprays also get the job done more efficiently. The handheld showerhead, *right,* provides quick rinse-offs after a tub bath.

■ **Sliding bar showerhead.** These showerheads, *above,* slide up and down on a bar mounted on the wall. Because the height of the spray is extremely easy to adjust, it's a good option when there is a significant variation in the heights of the people using the shower.

■ **Body spray and body mist shower sprays.** These heads or sprays are installed in vertical rows on opposite or adjacent walls, creating a crisscross water massage between the knee and shoulder levels that allows

# Bathtubs

Right: **Platform-style tubs are the most common style of whirlpool tubs sold. These tubs are installed in a fashion very similar to a self-rimming sink; the tub simply drops into a separate platform, making installation versatile.**

Most people who want to replace a bathtub are doing it because they either want a larger model or they are stepping up to a whirlpool. Before making such an investment, you and your family members should sit in the tub to make sure it fits. Likewise, you'll need to find out if the tub you want will actually fit in the space you are allocating for it as well as through your existing doorways. (Getting your old bathtub out of the house may also test your ingenuity and your patience.) If the tub you want won't fit through the doors, stairwells, and hallways that connect to your bathroom, your only choice will be to either downsize the tub or knock out an exterior wall.

Most bathroom floors can handle 40 pounds of weight per square foot. A large-capacity tub may require extra bracing so that the floor can support it once it is filled with water.

If you're installing a whirlpool, you'll also need to have access to the pump

## GETTING IN HOT WATER

The National Kitchen and Bath Association recommends that your hot water heater be at least two-thirds the capacity of your tub: a 60-gallon hot water tank will serve a 90-gallon tub adequately, but the rest of the water in your house will be cold. The tub's manual will tell you how many gallons of water it will take to fill it.

If your hot water heater is too small, you can either install a bigger heater or install two heaters side-by-side. You can also buy a whirlpool tub with an in-line heater of its own. Instead of heating water before use like a hot water tank, an inline heater maintains the temperature of the water for the duration of your bath. If you plan to soak for long periods, an in-line heater is a good idea regardless of the capacity of your hot water heater.

**BATHTUB REFINISHING**

For information on refinishing an existing tub, see page 64.

Left: **This unusually shaped tub fits into tight quarters. Finished only on one narrow, rounded end, the glass shower adjacent to the tub has an extra deep shower pan to prevent the tub's unfinished side from showing.**

(typically installed near one end of the tub) in case repairs are necessary. To make your whirlpool bath more soothing, choose a pump that is quiet and offers a wide range of massage options.

Both whirlpool and standard bathtubs come in four basic designs:

■ **Recessed tubs.** With one finished side called an apron, a recessed tub fits between two end walls and against a back wall. Models are available with a drain at either end to fit your plumbing needs. People with limited mobility may find it difficult to get in and out of these tubs.

■ **Corner tubs.** Space-saving corner tubs fit diagonally between two corners and, like standard apron tubs, have only one finished side. Other corner options are also similar to apron tubs, except the tubs have both a fin-

ished side and end, like the tub shown *above,* with one rounded, finished end.

■ **Freestanding tubs.** These tubs are finished on all four sides and can be placed most anywhere in the room. Freestanding clawfoot tubs, like the new tub on page 100, look great in traditional baths. You can also find freestanding tubs that have a more contemporary look.

■ **Platform tubs.** Like the one shown on *opposite,* these tubs have no finished panels; they are dropped into a platform. Platform tubs can be placed anywhere depending on the platform's design: into a corner, against a long wall, or in the center of the room.

Bathtub prices start at about $500 for a basic 5-foot model and can cost more than $3,000 for a high-end whirlpool.

## Materials:

■ **Enameled cast iron.** These tubs are made from iron molded into a bathtub shape and finished with enamel. They are thicker than the others and retain the heat of the water very well. Durable and solid, these tubs also come in a variety of color options. Cast-iron tubs are heavy, so you may need to reinforce the flooring below the tub.

■ **Enameled steel.** Produced by spraying enamel onto molded steel and firing the tub at a high temperature, these tubs are less expensive and not as heavy as their cast iron counterparts. These tubs do, however, chip more readily and have less color options. The tubs can also be noisier when being filled with water.

■ **Fiberglass.** Fiberglass backing material is finished with a layer of polyester to create this bathtub. Wood or metal reinforcement is then added to make the tub feel solid. Inexpensive, these tubs are available in a wide choice of styles and shapes, and are light in weight. The polyester finish is not as durable as acrylic, and the tubs do not retain heat well.

■ **Acrylic.** Sheets of acrylic are heated and formed in a mold, then reinforced with fiberglass and a wood or metal backing. These tubs are also available in a wide choice of styles and shapes, and are light in weight. More expensive than fiberglass, acrylic tubs hold heat better if properly insulated, but the finish can still scratch.

■ **Cast polymer.** Solid-color, polymer-based materials are used to create these tubs that are often made to resemble a natural stone, such as granite or marble. Thicker than acrylic, the tubs hold heat well. These tubs are covered in the same polyester gel as fiberglass tubs, so they are not as durable as either acrylic or enameled cast-iron tubs.

Below: **Finished all the way around, this clawfoot tub can be installed anywhere in the room because it's freestanding.**

Even the most basic tubs can feel luxurious in the right setting. A standard white, cast-iron tub takes on new glory by demurring to its surroundings.

# Fixtures

## Showers

**Above:** This roomy custom-made ceramic-tile shower is fitted with an acrylic plastic shower door and side panel.

**Above right:** A prefabricated neo-angle shower stall saves floor space and offers an attractive look.

When space and budget allow, including a separate shower in the bathroom layout is a luxurious choice. Separate fixtures mean two people can bathe at the same time. Shower stalls are also easier to get in and out of and easier to clean than combination tub/shower units. If space and budget are limited, make a combination unit safer by selecting a non-slip bottom and grab bars. There are three basic types of separate shower stalls:

■ **Prefabricated stalls.** Available in a wide variety of shapes and colors, these stalls are available in one-piece, two-piece, or three-piece versions. The most common material for these units is fiberglass with a finish surface of acrylic or other plastic. Tempered glass combined with fiberglass stalls is also available. Sizes range from 32 inches square (not large enough to meet some local codes) to 36x48 inches. One-piece versions are typically reserved for new construction and new additions. Like a bathtub or whirlpool, one-piece stalls are very large and can be difficult to get into the room. Two- and three-piece models readily fit within most door openings. Doors (or curtains) are typically sold separately. Some come with their own pan— or flooring piece—while others require a separate pan.

Prefabricated stalls are available in three shapes: square, rectangular, and neo-angle. They are designed to fit against a wall or into a corner. Corner or neo-angle models (like the one pictured *above*) have two sides and a diagonal front. Most prefabricated units are made of fiberglass finished with either an acrylic or polyester gel coat. The walls of the stall need to be attached to standard wall framing for support. Prefabricated stalls range in price from $300 (for acrylic) to $1,000 or more for glass.

■ **Prefabricated shower pans.** These molded flooring pieces are available in a range of materials from plastic to stone. They can be combined with prefabricated shower stalls, or custom-made acrylic plastic, solid-surface walls, or tiled shower walls. Prices start at about $75.

■ **Custom-made stalls.** These stalls offer the most design flexibility; there's no limit on the size or the style of a custom-made shower. Any waterproof material can be used for the walls, including tile, marble, solid-surfacing, tempered glass, or glass blocks.

### STEAM IT UP

Equip your shower stalls with a top and a door that seals tightly and you can use the stall as a steam bath. If you want to do this, you'll need to install a vapor barrier on the ceiling and wall framing to keep the moisture from reaching the studs and joists, and causing rot. You'll also need to have a steam generator installed somewhere outside the shower. This custom-designed shower has been fitted with steam generator, dual showerheads, and an adjustable handheld spray.

The shower *below* combines marble with tempered glass. Prices vary depending on materials used, as well as the size and complexity of the shower stall's design.

Left: **This custom shower stall takes advantage of all the options: arched opening and ceiling, unique shape, and deep windows. The components used to create this one-of-a-kind beauty, however, could all be standard. It's the assembly that makes a specialized statement.**

**A** toilet may be utilitarian, but that doesn't mean it can't be stylish. Design choices range from classic two-piece models, like the one shown *opposite,* to sleek low-profile single-piece models, as shown *below.*

Choose a toilet that fits both your comfort level and the look you are trying to create. Whether you are purchasing all new fixtures or just one, make sure the unit you select matches or complements the color and style of the other fixtures in your bath.

Models with elongated bowls as shown *below* are more comfortable and more expensive than standard round toilets. Toilet heights range from the standard 14 inches up to 17 inches high. The taller toilets are more comfortable for tall people or people with disabilities.

## The lowdown on low flow

By law, toilets manufactured after January 1, 1994, may use no more than 1.6 gallons of water per flush. Models manufactured before this date use 3.5 or more gallons per flush. Unfortunately, many of the low-flow models introduced in the mid-1990s did not work very well. Because of this, they often have to be flushed twice to get the job done, so they don't save much water.

Today's low-flow toilets work much better than those early models. There are three types of low-flow toilets:

■ **Gravity flush.** The least expensive of the low-flow options, these toilets work using the same principles as models produced before the low-flow mandate. The weight of the water flowing down from the tank clears the bowl. The water pressure in your neighborhood will affect how gravity-assisted

---

**EASY CLEANING**

Unbroken lines make one-piece toilets easier to clean than two-piece models. Wide bowls require less scrubbing than narrow ones because the wider design does a better job of clearing waste. Toilets with straight sides that hide the bolts that secure it to the floor are also easier to wipe clean than models with lots of lumps and bumps.

Right: **Sleek and with a low-profile, this toilet sleekly carries the room's sophisticated look.**

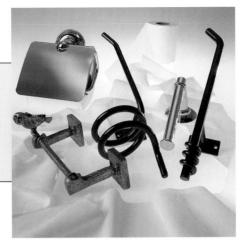

**WHERE TO PUT THE PAPER**

Perhaps the most overlooked of all bathroom hardware is the paper holder. These unusual versions add a little design flair to the utilitarian piece. Locate the holder within easy reach and view of the toilet.

toilets work. Most manufacturers recommend about 25 pounds per square inch to work best. (Your water pressure can also fluctuate with household activities, such as turning on the lawn sprinklers.) Relatively easy to install, these models do not discharge waste as effectively as the other two options. Prices start near $100.

■ **Pressure assisted.** When this toilet is flushed, pressurized air created from a vessel hidden in the toilet tank forces water into the bowl and down the drain. The most effective low-flow option, these toilets are noisier than gravity flush and are more expensive to repair. Prices for one-piece units with a pressure-assisted flush range from $300 to $600.

■ **Pump assisted.** These toilets eliminate waste with the assistance of an electric pump that propels water into the bowl and down the drain. These toilets are the most expensive of three. They work nearly as well as pressure-assisted toilets but without

making as much noise. Prices start out at around $500.

If you want to keep your current toilet, but would like to reduce its water consumption, you can displace some of the water in the tank by placing a water-filled plastic bottle into the tank. Or you can install a dual flusher that allows a half-flush for liquid-only flushes.

## The bidet

Although bidets are not used as widely in the United States as they are in Europe, they are gaining in popularity. The fixture resembles a toilet, but actually works more like a sink. Water ascends from the center of the bowl to rinse off the posterior of the person sitting on the bowl. Both genders can safely use a bidet.

Unlike a toilet, a bidet must be plumbed with both hot and cold water, as well as a drain. For convenience, locate the bidet close to the toilet. If the two fixtures are installed side by side, leave at least 15 inches between them. Expect the fixture to take up at least 3 square feet of floor space.

Left: **This attractive two-piece, traditionally styled toilet meets current low-flow flush requirements.**

### DESIGNER TIP

**If your bath accentuates angles, choose a toilet that echoes angular design. A room with curves and soft edges should have a toilet with the same characteristics. Color choices are extensive; choose a neutral color if you like to periodically change the decor. White and cream color toilets are less costly (and less likely to eventually look dated) than the same model in more vibrant colors.**

# Cabinetry Options

Below: **Attractive enough for a dining room, this bath vanity hutch stores numerous grooming supplies. The mirrored upper cabinet doors resemble glass but do not require neatness.**

The vanity area often serves as a focal point for your bathroom and helps define the entire design. The modest single-sink vanity cabinet has given way to a host of bathroom cabinetry options, from double-sink vanities, as shown on page 109, to custom storage hutches, as shown *below*. Bath cabinets are available in an ever-increasing array of style, material, and color choices. As with kitchen cabinets, you can purchase bath cabinets in modular (stock) units or you can have one custom-designed and built by a cabinet shop.

There is no rule against using kitchen cabinets in the bath; the only difference is that vanity cabinets are typically 29 to 30 inches high while kitchen base cabinets are typically 36 inches high. Similarly, vanity cabinets' front-to-back depth is 18 to 21 inches, while the front-to-back depth of kitchen cabinets typically runs 24 inches deep. Many people find the 36-inch height

Left: Turn empty wall space into storage by recessing shelves into stud space. This storage unit goes one step further: The center portion pulls out of its frame to reveal understair storage for holiday decorations and other seldom-used items.

more comfortable for standing. If the people who share the bathroom are of significantly different heights, you may want to customize the height of each vanity (or vanity section).

Most standard, also called stock, vanities run 18 inches front to back. Widths start out at 18 inches and continue in 6-inch increments to 72 inches. Matching filler pieces can be used to adapt a standard vanity to fit most any space. Semicustom cabinets are similar to stock cabinets in that these cabinet lines offer standard styles and finishes, but increased size options, usually within 3-inch increments, are offered. Cabinets designed and built specifically for the bath where they will be used are called custom.

When planning your vanity, allow enough room in the front of the vanity for the doors and drawers to open and close without interference. There should be

## HARDWARE

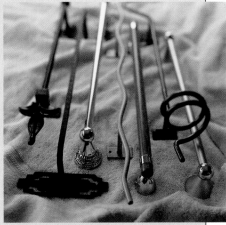

Often overlooked in bath planning, pretty hardware accessorizes a bath like fine jewels do an evening gown. Choices are endless as are the price ranges attached to them.

To find just the right cabinetry knobs, search catalogs, home improvement stores, and the Internet. Playful pieces are ideal for children's baths, while more sophisticated pulls look great in master or guest baths.

When it comes to choosing a towel bar, choose a sturdy model that will hold as many towels as you need. Install multiple rings to hold multiple towels. Don't forget to include a robe hook; the terry wrap that hangs on it is typically the second thing you reach for after bathing.

Small pieces such as soap dishes, tissue and toilet paper dispensers, tumblers and swab holders also pack personality into a bathroom. Choose models that complement the remainder of your hardware.

Right: Design your bath like you would any living space and you immediately open yourself up to new decorating options. This glass-fronted hutch serves as an attractive, functional storage piece in this country-comfortable bath.

enough wall space for a mirror and light fixtures. If either side of the vanity is exposed and a corner juts out into the room, consider curved edges to prevent painful bumps from occurring.

Plan for the amount of storage you will need by making a list of the specific items you will store there, from toiletries and curling irons to towels, cleaning supplies, and toilet paper.

How the cabinets are made and what the cabinets are made from has a direct bearing on the price. Solid wood components are more expensive and more durable than veneered woods glued over fiberboard.

Bath cabinet prices range from $35 to $160 per linear foot, including installation.

### Store more.

Add convenience to your dressing routine by allocating some bath drawers for storage of undergarments and sleepwear. Instead of adding a closet or more built-in cabinets, increase bath storage by including free-standing furniture pieces, such as a chest of drawers, into your bath's design. The old-fashioned hutch, *above*, holds a plethora of bath linens and toiletries. Maximize each piece's storage capacity by customizing the shelves inside to fit the exact items you plan to store.

## Be creative.

Bring a jewelry box into the bath and fill it with cosmetics and hair accessories. Use glass shelves to fill empty wall space behind a tub or toilet. Fill recessed stud space with medicine cabinets or open shelves. Add an open storage and display hutch between two existing sinks, as shown *below*. Plan open storage niches for neat, yet handy, storage.

Far left: **The niche keeps facial towels handy while adding an elegant touch to the bath cabinet's design.**
Left: **Linen storage never looked so good. This flea-market-find corner cabinet fits so neatly in this small bath that it looks as though it's always been there.**
Below: **Instead of one large mirror above this double vanity, two smaller ones leave enough wall space for an attractive, open storage hutch.**

### DESIGNER TIP

For more storage ideas, see Storage Strategies on pages 122–125.

# Elements of Good Design

Once you have your material and fixture selections in mind, it's time to get down to the nitty gritty job of fitting it all comfortably into the space you have.

Remodeling success is measured in terms of comfort, function, and personal style. Ergonomics—the characteristics of people that need to be considered when arranging your fixtures—plays a significant role in bath design. So do plumbing layouts—the number of walls in your bath that will need to have water pipes behind them—and safety. You'll also need to plan for proper lighting, ventilation, conservative water usage, and noise reduction. Here, you'll find more ways to add privacy to a shared space, plus ways to make the storage you have work harder, all while ensuring your bath is as easy on the eyes as it is on the body.

Opposite: **By following the National Kitchen and Bath Association recommendations for minimum clearances, you ensure your bath will comfortably fit the needs of most people. Leaving an aisle that is at least 3 feet wide, for example, ensures that people of all sizes can pass comfortably through your bath. When it comes to counter space, leave at least 8 inches of space between the edge of the sink and the end of the counter.**

# Minimum Clearances

Based on average human measurements and needs, professional designers have developed recommendations for minimum clearance around doors, fixtures, cabinets, and other common bathroom elements. The following guidelines as outlined by the National Kitchen and Bath Association (NKBA) should work well for anyone at any stage of life, although some of these dimensions will need to be larger for a completely barrier-free bath, as described on pages 114–115. Keep in mind that these are the recommended minimums, not hard and fast rules; allow more space if the fit seems tight for any of the bathroom's intended users.

## Floor space guidelines

Clear floor spaces required at each fixture may overlap. That is, you can add the clear space between a toilet and a tub together, just make sure that the amount of space between the two meets the minimum guidelines for both.

■ **Door openings.** All doorways should be at least 32 inches wide. Allow a clear floor space at least the width of the door on the push side and a larger clear floor space on the pull side to allow enough room for bath users to comfortably open, close, and pass through the doorway.

■ **Walkways.** Make passages between the walls and fixtures at least 36 inches wide.

■ **Sink fronts.** Leave at least 30x48 inches (either parallel or perpendicular) of clear floor space in front of each sink. If there is open knee space under the sink, up to 12 of the 48 inches can extend beneath the sink.

■ **Toilet allowance.** Leave a clear floor space of 48x48 inches in front of the toilet. If floor area is limited, a 30x48-inch space may be adequate. Leave at least 16 inches of space from the centerline of the fixture to the closest fixture or sidewall. Allow at least 1 inch between the back of the water tank and the wall behind it. If you plan to install a toilet in its own separate compartment, make the compartment at least 36 inches wide and 66 inches long. Install a swing-out door or a pocket door on the opening to the compartment. The doorway should be at least 32 inches wide.

■ **Bidet allowance.** Leave a clear floor space of 48x48 inches in front of the bidet. Leave at least 16 inches of space from the centerline of the fixture to the closest fixture or sidewall. When the toilet and bidet are adjacent, maintain the 16 inches of minimum clearance to all obstructions.

■ **Bathtub entrance.** Plan a 30x60-inch section of clear space adjacent to the tub if you'll approach the fixture from the side.

Below: **Leave at least 30x48 inches (either parallel or perpendicular) of clear floor space in front of each sink. If there is open knee space under the sink (such as in this pedestal version), up to 12 inches of the 48 inches can extend beneath the sink. Plan clear floor space in front of the shower that is 36 inches deep and as wide as the shower.**

Leave 48x60 inches of clear floor space if you'll approach the fixture from the front.

■ **Shower entrance.** For showers less than 60 inches wide, plan a clear floor space that is 36 inches deep and 12 inches wider than the shower. For wider showers, plan for a clear floor space that is 36 inches deep and as wide as the shower.

■ **Shower interior.** The minimum usable interior dimensions, measured from wall to wall, are 34x34 inches, but most people prefer it roomier. If there simply isn't enough space, you can reduce this to 32x32 inches, but it may make the shower uncomfortable for some users. Design the shower doors so that they open into the bathroom—not into the stall—to avoid crowding the space in the shower.

### Grooming space guidelines

These NKBA guidelines ensure that everyone in the bath has adequate grooming space and elbowroom near the sink, vanities, and countertops.

■ **Sink space.** Leave at least 15 inches of clearance from the centerline of a sink to the closest sidewall. If you are including two sinks in a vanity, leave at least 30 inches of clearance between the centerlines of each. If the sinks are wider than 30 inches, increase the distance by several inches to provide a minimum of 8 inches of open counter space between the sinks to allow adequate elbowroom when both sinks are in use.

■ **Vanity height.** If you are including two vanities, make them different heights—one between 30 and 34 inches high and one between 34 and 42 inches high—to match the comfort level of the people that use them. Vanity cabinets are typically 29 to 30 inches high, while kitchen base cabinets are typically 36 inches high. Many people find the 36-inch height more comfortable for standing. If space allows, add a 30-inch-high section with knee space below for sitting.

■ **Mirror height.** Locate a mirror above a vanity so that its bottom edge is no more than 40 inches above the floor. If the top of the mirror is tilted away from the wall, its bottom edge can be as much as 48 inches above the floor.

■ **Door and drawer widths.** When designing a vanity cabinet, split doors in cabinets that are 24 inches or wider. Large single doors can be awkward to open, especially in a narrow bathroom. Avoid narrow doors and drawers. Nine-inch widths are too narrow to be extremely useful.

■ **Corner comfort.** To eliminate sharp corners, use countertops with rounded corners and eased edges.

Above: **Provide a minimum of 8 inches—12 inches is better—of open counter space between the sinks in a double vanity to allow adequate elbowroom when both sinks are in use. Locate the mirror above the vanity no more than 40 inches above the floor so that people of varying heights can comfortably use it. Use only GFCI switches near the vanity to reduce the risk of electrical shock.**

### DESIGNER TIP

**For more information about the NKBA, you can visit the NKBA's website at www.nkba.org or call 877/NKBAPRO.**

# Barrier-Free Baths

The goal of a barrier-free bath is to make all users as independent and as comfortable as possible. Even if no one in your home has special needs now, planning a bath that can accommodate wheelchairs and walkers can make guests—or even a kid with a cast—feel more welcome and more comfortable.

■ **Location, location, location.** Creating a barrier-free bath starts first with the room's location. It should be situated on the home's ground floor so that there are no stairs to climb up or down.

■ **Door size.** Plan for a clear door opening of 34 inches; larger openings are difficult to open and close from a seated position and narrower openings make it difficult, if not impossible, for a wheelchair to make it through.

■ **Handle selection.** Equip entrance doors, drawers, and faucets with lever or D-shape handles. They are easier to operate than knobs, especially for young children and people with arthritis or limited mobility.

■ **Floor space.** For a typical-size wheelchair to make a complete turnaround, you'll need to leave a circular area of clear floor space measuring 5 feet in diameter. Leave an area in front of the sink that measures at least 30x48 inches (although the clear floor space can overlap). Toilets need a clear floor space that is 48 inches square. Bathtubs need a clear floor space of 60x60 inches in front of the tub.

■ **Shower stalls.** Shower stalls are easier to get in and out of than bathtubs. Choose a stall with no curb or a very short one. Slope the floor toward the drain to ensure that the water stays within the enclosure. Shower stalls need to measure at least 4 feet square with an opening that is at least 36 inches wide. Include a built-in bench or seat that is 17 to 19 inches above the floor, grab bars, a single-handle lever control, and a handheld shower spray.

■ **Bathtubs.** If a tub is a necessity, install grab bars in the tub along the side wall and the two end walls. Install the bars 33 to 36 inches above the tub bottom and another set 9 inches above the tub rim. All bars should be at least 24 inches long.

■ **Knee space.** The knee space under a sink should be about 27 inches high and 30 inches wide. In addition, hot water pipes should be insulated or concealed to protect users from scalding.

■ **Toilet talk.** The ideal placement for a toilet is in a corner of the bath so that you can install grab bars both behind the toilet and next to it. Leave at least 48 inches of clear floor space to either one side or in front of the toilet. A toilet 3 inches higher than a conventional model makes it easier to transfer to or from a wheelchair. As a general rule, grab bars should be 33 to 36 inches above the floor. They should be 42 inches long on a side wall and not more than 12 inches from the back wall. The bar on the back wall should be at least 24 inches long and extend at least 12 inches from each side of the center of the toilet.

**Below: This traditional-style bath provides for drive-in grooming. Narrow drawers on both sides of the sink keep toothbrushes and other toiletries handy. A rug-look pattern in the nonslip blue and white tile flooring adds warmth without inhibiting wheelchair maneuverability.**

**BARRIER-FREE INFORMATION**

• Barrier-Free Environments, P.O. Box 30634; Raleigh, NC 27633; 919/782-7823
• Abledata, 8630 Fenton Street, Suite 930; Silver Spring, MD 20910; 800/227-0216; www.abledata.com

■ **Grab bars.** Rated to withstand up to 300 pounds of pressure, grab bars are efficient only if they are attached securely. Secure grab bars to wall studs, or if possible, before putting up drywall, install ¾-inch plywood sheathing over the studs from floor to ceiling. You can then install bars anywhere on the walls as needed. Buy bars with a nonslip texture. They come in a variety of colors and styles to blend with most any bath decor.

■ **Windows.** Casement windows are the easiest to operate from a wheelchair. Install windows 24 to 30 inches above the floor so that wheelchair users can open, close, and easily see out of them.

Above: **A simple ramp makes entrance to this accessible shower easier than trying to drive over the threshold. Clear space in front of the tub enables a wheelchair user to transfer from chair to tub and back again. The front-mount tub faucets present easy accessibility from both inside and outside the tub.**

## FOR SAFETY'S SAKE

• **Grab bars.** Reinforce walls for grab bars at the time of construction. Install grab bars in the tub, shower, and toilet areas.

• **GFCI outlets.** Protect all receptacles, lights, and switches in the room with ground fault circuit interrupters (GFCIs) to reduce the risk of electrical shocks. Install only moisture-proof light fixtures above the tub and shower areas.

• **Flooring grip.** Install only slip-resistant flooring throughout the entire bath area. Choose rugs with nonskid backing, and install rubber foot pads on all step stools and vanity chairs to prevent them from slipping when in use.

• **Shower and tub surround safety.** Include a bench or a seat that is 17 to 19 inches above the floor and at least 15 inches deep. It can be a hanging or folding seat; to support the seat, you will need to reinforce the wall when you install the surround. To reduce the risk of falls, avoid installing steps for climbing into the shower or tub. Design the surround so that you can reach the controls from inside and outside the stall. Put the controls 38 to 48 inches above the floor and above the grab bar if there is one. Locate the controls between the showerhead and the stall door. For a handheld showerhead model, locate the head no higher than 48 inches above the floor when in its lowest position. To help prevent cuts and bruises, add a cushion to the tub spout. (Waterproof cushions in various shapes are readily available at many bath and hardware centers.) Install only laminated safety glass with a plastic inner layer, tempered glass, or approved plastic for any clear face of a shower or tub enclosure or partition that reaches to within 18 inches of the floor.

• **Water safety.** Turn your hot water heater down to 120 degrees. Or install a pressure-balancing/temperature regulator or a temperature-limiting device for all faucet heads, particularly showerheads, to prevent scalding. To prevent drowning, never leave a small child unattended in the bathtub. Keep washcloths and toys at tubside, so you won't be tempted to walk away for any reason. Install a childproof latch on the toilet lid. Round countertop and cabinetry corners.

• **Safety latches.** Finally, if you EVER have young children in your house, install childproof locks on all cabinets.

# The Right Light

Proper bath lighting provides shadowless, glare-free illumination throughout the room. Plan for a blend of at least two different illumination strategies: ambient and task lighting. You should also consider including a third type of illumination: accent lighting.

Above: **These surface-mounted "Hollywood" lights installed above and on both sides of the mirror provide excellent task lighting for applying makeup and shaving.**

Ambient or general lighting creates a uniform, overall glow in the entire bath space and comes from one or more, usually overhead, sources. (If your bath is larger than 35 square feet, one overhead fixture will not be enough.) Backing up this general lighting plan is task lighting. These fixtures are positioned to eliminate shadows in the areas where you perform specific tasks such as applying makeup, shaving, or taking a bath. Accent lighting occurs when you aim light on an object or surface simply to show it off. For this job, you'll need a lightbulb—or lamp—with a beam that is three to five times brighter than the general lighting lamps. To learn what types of lighting are inherently brighter, take a look at what's available in incandescent, fluorescent, or halogen bulbs, *opposite bottom,* then pair them with an almost endless variety of fixture styles.

## Fixture styles

There are many fixture choices. You will likely need a combination of styles to fully light your bath.

- **Recessed downlights.** Also called can lights, these lights are very popular and the least-obtrusive fixture for general or task lighting. For best ambient lighting, position these lights close enough together so that their light patterns overlap.
- **Pendant lights.** Lights that hang from a wire or chain can work well in the bathroom, either as overall ambient light or placed over the vanity for task light. If you have a large traditional-style bath, a small chandelier can also give the bath the look and feel of living space as opposed to utility room.
- **Surface-mounted fixtures.** These fixtures work well in bathrooms that cannot accommodate recessed fixtures, a common problem in bath remodelings. Available in many styles and sizes, there are surface-mounted fixtures for either incandescent or fluorescent bulbs.
- **Wall sconces.** To create ambient lighting, use wall sconces throughout the bath. Wall sconces placed on both sides of a mirror offer shadow free task light for applying makeup or shaving.
- **Shower-safe fixtures.** For safety purposes, shower fixtures like the one shown *opposite* should always be waterproof and steamproof; most building codes require this.
- **Rheostats.** Also called dimmers, these light-regulating knobs or levers enable you to set the fixture at any level of light from a soft glow that backs up a candlelit bath to radiant brightness for cleaning the tub afterward. Dimmers are also energy savers as they enable you to use only the amount of light you need and not more.

daylight spectrum range. Avoid choosing bulbs that are too white or too yellow in color as the mirror won't reflect a true picture of how you look outside the bathroom.

## Lighting the shower and tub

In an enclosed shower or tub area, most building codes require enclosed, vapor-proof downlights. Place the fixtures so that they fully light the tub or shower but don't shine directly in your eyes when you're relaxing in the tub. All light switches should be located at least 6 feet from a tub or shower.

## Stall lighting

One centrally located fixture, installed in the ceiling or high on the wall, should be enough to adequately light a shower stall.

## Night-lights

Night-lights make those late-night or early-morning trips to the bathroom more comfortable for people of all ages. For an easy, affordable solution, plug in an automatic night-light that senses the amount of light coming into the room. Or install a low-voltage system below the vanity toe kick or around some shelving to provide soft night-time illumination.

Left: **This surface-mounted light fixture is waterproof and steamproof, and can be mounted on either the wall or the ceiling of a shower.**

## Lighting the mirror

Because your bathroom mirror serves as the primary grooming center in the house, make sure it is evenly illuminated and free of shadows. To do this, light sources need to be placed so that the light is evenly distributed from above, below, and both sides. This cross-lighting prevents shadows from appearing, which make applying makeup evenly very difficult. "Movie star" lights, the kind you see in the dressing rooms of actors, surround the entire mirror with bulbs and are the ideal lighting solution for perfect makeup application.

If that is not the look you are after, then plan to install one or two fixtures above the mirror that cast light just over the front edge of the sink and the countertop. Add two additional lights centered on each side of the mirror. If there is not enough space at the sides of the mirror for fixtures, you can create cross-lighting by making the light above the mirror longer than the width of the mirror itself. Choose a light color, preferably white, countertop so that more light reflects on your face.

Always select bulbs designed for vanity illumination: these bulbs create light in the

---

**BULB BASICS**

- **Incandescent.** Introduced by Thomas Edison back in 1879, incandescent bulbs are still widely used and appreciated for the white light they offer, and because more energy-efficient, longer lasting incandescents are available today. Low-voltage incandescent fixtures make good accent lighting. Operating on 12 or 24 volts, these lights require transformers, which are sometimes built into the fixture to step down the voltage from standard 120-volt household circuits.
- **Fluorescent.** Fluorescent tubes are energy efficient and last far longer than incandescent bulbs. Today's tubes reduce noise and flicker and come in a wide spectrum of colors. New subcompact tubes can be used in fixtures that usually require incandescent bulbs.
- **Halogen.** Quartz halogen lights offer bright, white light good for task or accent lighting. Usually low-voltage, these bulbs do put off a large amount of heat. Choose a fixture specifically designed for halogen bulbs.

# Windows and Skylights

Proper lighting goes beyond choosing the right fixtures; it also includes bringing in as much natural light as possible with skylights, glass doors, wall cutouts, glass block, and windows. Mirrors also reflect and increase the amount of natural light that enters your bath.

Skylights offer an ideal way to bring daylight into a bath, providing your bath's location allows for it. To prevent moisture and condensation problems, choose a high-quality model and install it according to the manufacturer's specifications.

Think beyond the outdated notion of using a single double-hung window. Look for places to install additional windows where they will shed more light in the vanity area without looking out of place on your home's exterior. Consider installing a frosted-glass door or an open cutout between the master bath and bedroom to let light filter from one room into the other.

## Ventilation

Without proper ventilation, the ceiling may mildew, the wallpaper may curl, the paint may peel, and the mirror may even begin to deteriorate. Open windows when you can and supplement them with a high-quality fan.

To determine the size of venting fan you need, measure your bath's cubic feet (width times length times ceiling height) and multiply the result by 8, then divide by 60. The result is the minimum cubic feet per minute (cfm) rating you'll need in a venting fan. The noise from a fan will resonate on the hard surfaces of a bathroom, so choose a quiet fan that vents to the outside with a noise level not exceeding 3 sones; less than 2 sones is highly recommended.

Right: **A trio of operable double-hung windows combines with a decorative round-top window above them to open up this bath to natural light, ventilation, and tranquil waterfront views.**

## Water conservation

Clean, fresh water is a renewable resource, but we must use it wisely to keep supply and demand at an equilibrium. All states now require that newly installed toilets be low-flow fixtures. (See pages 104–105 for more information on low-flow toilets.)

Showers are another heavy water user. Low-flow showerheads restrict water output to 2.5 gallons of water per minute. That's 30 to 60 percent less than an average shower-head output. The technology of water-saving showerheads has improved to the point where many of today's low-cost models seem just as generous with water as their older higher-consuming counterparts. Flow-restricting aerators on sink faucets aid conservation still further. All these low-flow fixtures are available in hardware stores, home centers, and bath fixture shops.

Above: **Operable skylights provide sunlight and ventilation in this attic bath without sacrificing privacy.**

## Filtration systems

Water that contains a significant amount of iron, sulfur, lime, and other mineral impurities is commonly referred to as hard water. Hard water can irritate the skin, causing itching and dryness, particularly in the winter months when the air is drier. Hard water also causes unsightly deposits on your fixtures and can affect how well your shampoos and soaps lather.

Bacteria, nitrates, lead, and other conta-minants can make your water unsafe for drinking. Do-it-yourself water-testing kits that cost about $20 (available at home centers and via the Internet) can check for both hardness and contamination. If your water test shows problems other than hardness, contact your local water municipality immediately to determine what steps you need to take. A water purification system may be necessary. If your water is determined to be hard, you might want to invest in a water

**Above:** Tucked into an alcove, this bathtub receives natural light from two different directions. Roman shades control the amount of light and privacy.

softener. Softened water requires less soap for bathing and your plumbing system will work more smoothly because your water heater, pipes, showerheads, and faucets won't collect the corrosive scale that hard water causes.

## Easy cleaning

Including some of these features into your bath will prevent your dream bath from becoming a cleaning nightmare.

■ **Cut down on wiping up.** Consider fog-free mirrors and automatic or lever-handle faucets. Choose nonporous stone, laminate, or solid-surface walls, floors, and countertops. The fewer the seams, nooks, or crannies, the better. Curving your countertop up the wall creates a seamless backsplash that eliminates the dirt-catching right-angle joint where the counter meets the wall. In front, make sure the countertop edge overhangs the cabinet doors or drawers somewhat, otherwise spills may get into the cabinets of seep into drawers. Likewise, the fewer the seams or gaps in your floor, the fewer the places for dirt and hair to collect. Eliminate the seam between the base cabinet and the vertical surface of the toe kick by "rolling" the edge of the floor up to the top of the toe kick, replacing the right angle joint with a smooth curve. The technique is easiest with vinyl, linoleum, or tile, but it is also possible with wood if you have the edge pieces custom milled.

■ **Reduce mildew.** To keep germs and mildew at bay, look for the following products: moisture-resistant tile underlayment, mildew-resistant tile grout, mildew-resistant wall paint, and antibacterial or bacteria-inhibiting features (some manufacturers of shower stalls and tub surrounds, for example, incorporate microban protection into their gel-coated interiors).

■ **Choose an easy-clean sink.** How your sink is attached to the countertop affects ease of cleaning. Integral sinks have no seams.

Undermount sinks are attached to the underside of a countertop. Both integral and undermount types make it easy to wipe messes from the counter right into the sink. Self-rimming sinks, on the other hand, have a perimeter lip that's sealed with a bead of caulk that can be a dirt collector.

■ **Choose grime-fighting cabinets.** Cabinets that have flat doors with a baked-on finish are easiest to clean. Stained cabinets with a flat or no-gloss finish don't show as much dirt, but they are more easily marred and harder to touch up. Elaborate cabinetry molding is harder to clean. Choose cabinet pulls and handles that keep you from getting the cabinet surface dirty instead of doors and drawers that you have to reach under to open. D-shape pulls work nicely; they let you open the door or drawer with one finger. In drawers that contain potentially messy items, such as toothpaste and lipstick tubes, install removable acrylic liners that can be thrown into the dishwasher when they become soiled.

# Storage Strategies

The key to keeping a bath neat and tidy is to make putting something away as easy as leaving it out on the counter. Being organized saves you time, space, and money while adding simplicity to your life.

■ **Take inventory.** To have enough room for everything you need, you need to get rid of what you never use. Sort through those bottles at the back of the cabinet and throw out what you never use or don't like. Some products, such as suntan lotions and face creams, have expiration dates. Throw out items that have expired and start out fresh.

■ **Designate a specific place** for each and every thing. You'll be more likely to put things back where they belong and less likely to unknowingly duplicate items if you know exactly where each item belongs.

■ **Store it where you use it.** Whenever pos-

**Below:** A pullout bin fitted with removable storage tubs keeps hair supplies neat. The tub could also serve as a mobile storage center for cleaning supplies.

Left: A simple tilt-out drawer can reduce countertop clutter and keep electrical outlets under wrap.
Below: This shallow, narrow cabinet fills what might have been unused space beside a vanity sink.

sible, you should store items right where they are used. For example, store your hair dryer in an appliance garage where you can keep it plugged in and ready to use. Store your toothbrush, toothpaste, and mouth-wash close enough to the sink so that you can grab them without even looking or taking a step away from the sink.

■ **Assign everything else a space** based on frequency of use. Store those electric rollers you only use for special occasions at the back of the cabinet or in a pantry cabinet down the hall. Store your cleaning supplies below the sink.

Above: **A tiled recess in the shower stall keeps soaps and towels handy.** Above right: **Pullout drawers reduce reaches and keep towels nearby. A built-in hamper provides a handy spot for dirty clothes.**

■ **Keep it simple.** When you have to open a door, stoop down, and reach to the back of a base cabinet to get to something you use every day, chances are you won't take the time to put it away when you're finished using it. Store the items you use frequently in the most convenient locations so that you will be more inclined to put them away.

■ **Make it comfortable.** It is easier on your back to reach into a drawer and grab a towel than it is to bend down and pull one out of a cabinet. Small vanity drawers, however, may only be big enough to hold one spare towel. Consider installing pullouts, like those shown *above,* for towel storage. For safety purposes, store heavier items in the lower spots, and lighter items in the high ones.

■ **Put wasted space to work.** Equip false sink fronts with pull-down baskets to hold toothpastes, razors, and other small items. Cut a niche between wall studs to hold perfume bottles, lotions, and powders. Add narrow shelves to the back side of base cabinet doors to hold additional lightweight toiletry items.

■ **Add a parking place.** Add a built-in bench where you can sit and pull on socks and shoes. Install drawers below the bench to hold socks and undergarments so you can quickly dress after a bath or shower.

■ **Create a spot for dirty clothes.** Is your bath situated next to the laundry room? If so, install a small top-swing door between the two rooms so you can toss clothes direct-

Left: These turntables enable you to find what you need at the spin of a wheel. Below: This built-in bath hutch has the look of furniture and stores plenty.

ly into a hamper stored on the laundry room side. If the laundry is below the bath, add a clothes chute so you don't have to tote dirty laundry down the stairs. If neither of these is an option, add a built-in hamper that is large enough to store the amount of dirty clothes that usually gather before you wash a load.

■ **Commit to a clutter-free bath.** Once you have your belongings in your cabinets, you'll have to work to keep the new system in place. Don't fill every single spot; keep a few drawers open for new items. If storage space is limited, follow this rule: one new thing in, one old thing out.

# Working with Professionals

Once you have carefully thought through your bath plans, you're heading into the homestretch. Before you begin the construction work, here are a few details you'll need to know about the process.

Hiring a skilled, dependable contractor is the most important step toward carrying out your remodeling plan in a timely, gratifying, and cost-effective manner. There are several kinds of contractors, so you'll want to match your remodeling needs with the capabilities of the people you hired to handle the project. Remodeling workers fall into four general categories:

■ **Repair workers.** These are the jacks-of-all-trades who do a little bit of everything from carpentry to minor plumbing and painting. These workers can be just right for small jobs, such as replacing a door or adding a window. They charge less per hour than specialized tradespeople.

■ **Tradespeople.** When you have a larger remodeling project but one that involves only a single trade, such as plumbing, electrical work, or carpentry, you can save money by hiring these tradespeople yourself. If you are interested in just a new sink, for example, hire a reputable plumber. Most skilled tradespeople can handle the entire job themselves even if there's a little carpentry involved. If they don't have the tools to do the entire job, most can let you know who else you need to contact.

■ **General contractors.** For projects that require more specialized tradespeople, you may want to hire a general remodeling contractor. This person or company will manage the entire project from start to finish. You'll get a single bid, and you won't have to worry

Right: **This simple-looking, handsome bath took a team of professionals to create: an architect and a designer; and building, plumbing, and electrical contractors. Without any one of them, the result would likely not have been as functional and pleasing.**